W9-BUT-578

THE PRIEST IN
CRISIS

THE PRIEST IN CRISIS / *a study in role change*

DAVID P. O'NEILL

 PFLAUM PRESS
DAYTON, OHIO
1968

Nihil Obstat: Eugene H. Maly
          Censor Deputatus, Jan. 8, 1968

Imprimatur: ✠ Edward A. McCarthy
          Vicar-General
          Archdiocese of Cincinnati, Jan. 10, 1968

The *Nihil Obstat* and the *Imprimatur* are official declarations that a book or pamphlet is free of doctrinal or moral error. No implication is contained therein that those who have granted the *Nihil Obstat* and the *Imprimatur* agree with the opinions expressed.

Library of Congress Catalog Card Number: 68-21240

Copyright © 1968 by David P. O'Neill

Printed in the United States of America

ACKNOWLEDGMENTS

The author acknowledges the use of the following copyrighted material.

Excerpts from the constitutions and decrees of the Ecumenical Council are taken from *The Documents of Vatican II*, published by Guild Press, America Press, Association Press, and Herder and Herder, and copyrighted 1966 by the America Press. Used by permission.

Harvey Cox, *The Secular City*, copyright © Harvey Cox 1965, The Macmillan Company, New York.

Terence Eagleton, *The New Left Church*, with permission of Helicon Press, Inc., Baltimore, Maryland and Sheed & Ward Ltd., London.

Erik H. Erikson, *Insight and Responsibility*, W. W. Norton & Co., Inc., of New York and Faber and Faber Limited, of London.

Joseph II. Fichter, *Religion as an Occupation*, with the permission of the University of Notre Dame Press.

Sigmund Freud, *An Outline of Psycho-analysis*, W. W. Norton & Co., Inc., of New York; Sigmund Freud Copyrights Ltd.; The Institute of Psycho-Analysis and Mrs. Alix Strachey; and The Hogarth Press Ltd. of London.

William F. Lynch, *Images of Hope*, Helicon Press, Inc., Baltimore, Maryland.

Marie Augusta Neal, *Values and Interest in Social Change*, © 1965. Reprinted by permission of Prentice-Hall, Inc., Englewood Cliffs, New Jersey.

David P. O'Neill, *About Loving*, copyright by the National Center of the Confraternity of Christian Doctrine, Washington, D.C.

Karl Rahner, *Bishops: Their Status and Function*, with permission of Helicon Press, Inc., Baltimore, Maryland and Burns & Oates Ltd., London.

Carl Rogers, *On Becoming a Person*, Houghton Mifflin Company of Boston.

Milton Rokeach, *The Open and Closed Mind*, Basic Books, Inc., Publishers, New York, 1960.

Daniel Callahan, *The Mind of the Catholic Layman*, Charles Scribner's Sons of New York.

Paul Tillich, *The Shaking of the Foundations*, Charles Scribner's Sons of New York and SCM Press Ltd., of London.

W. J. Sprott, *Human Groups*, Penguin Books of Harmondsworth, England.

Josef Goldbrunner, *Realization,* with the permission of the University of Notre Dame Press.
H. H. Gerth and C. Wright Mills, editors, *From Max Weber: Essays in Sociology,* Oxford University Press of New York.
Marshall McLuhan, *Understanding Media,* Copyright 1964 © by Marshall McLuhan. Used by permission of McGraw-Hill Book Company.
Robert W. Marks, editor, *Space, Time, and the New Mathematics,* copyright © 1964, by Bantam Books, Inc.
Karl W. Deutsch for material in *Space, Time, and the New Mathematics,* published by Bantam Books, which originally appeared in *The Nerves of Government* published by Free Press, New York.
Ronald Goldman, *Readiness for Religion,* Seabury Press of New York and Routledge & Kegan Paul Limited of London.
David P. O'Neill, *Priestly Celibacy and Maturity,* © Sheed & Ward, Inc., New York, 1965.
Louis Monden, *Sin, Liberty and Law,* © Sheed & Ward, Inc., New York, 1965.
John L. McKenzie, *Authority in the Church,* © Sheed & Ward, Inc., New York, 1966.
Harvey Cox, "The Revolt in the Church," in *Playboy,* January, 1967.
Ivan Illich, "The Vanishing Clergyman," from *The Critic,* June–July, 1967, copyright the Thomas More Association, Chicago, Illinois.
Rosemary Ruether, "Catholicism's Celibacy Crisis," copyright 1966, Christian Century Foundation. Reprinted by permission from the October 19, 1966, issue of *The Christian Century.*
John L. McKenzie, "Key Words in Scripture-Law" in *Living Light,* Winter, 1966–67.
David P. O'Neill, "The New Zealand Ombudsman," reprinted with permission from *America,* The National Catholic Weekly Review, 106 W. 56 Street, New York, New York 10019, copyright © 1965, America Press, Inc.
Charles Davis's editorial in *The Clergy Review,* July, 1966.
A. E. C. W. Spencer, "The Catholic Church and Communication," *The Clergy Review,* December, 1966.
Eugene Fontinell, "Reflections on Faith and Metaphysics," in *Cross Currents,* Winter, 1966.
Philip Scharper, "Frontiers of Theology," in *Theology Digest,* Winter, 1966.
The scripture quotations are in the translation of Monsignor Ronald Knox, copyright 1944, 1948 and 1950, Sheed & Ward, Inc., New York. With the kind permission of His Eminence the Cardinal Archbishop of Westminster.

CONTENTS

INTRODUCTION

This book has grown out of the many discussions on the Roman Catholic priesthood in which I have taken part over the past few years. Particularly since I wrote a book on the maturity and celibacy of priests, I have been asked to speak to many groups of priests and students for the priesthood, and have led them in seminars and discussions. Many Catholic lay people have talked to me about the crises surrounding the priestly role in the Church; they have given me the challenge of their insight and suggestions. Many psychologists and sociologists have discussed with me some of the ideas and suggestions in my previous books and articles; they have set my mind moving in new directions. Out of all this has grown a book—in a way, it is a record of myself in my searching, discussing, reading and observing over the past few years.

At the end of 1966, I found that I had been a priest for twenty-five years. At a small dinner to celebrate this unremarkable event, some of my friends urged me to write a book which would open up discussion on some of the problems and crisis areas of priestly life today; they spoke particularly about the rapidly changing role of the priest in the new Church growing around us. They asked me to write, not as a preacher or a theologian, but as one deeply involved in a changing role, one who has been seeing this evolution from the viewpoint of his daily life and work.

This, then, is not a sociological study of priests, like the schol-

arly research works of Fichter. It is not, either, a psychological
essay, such as you would find in the learned books of Rogers,
Erikson or Maslow. It is not, I think, a personal cry of witness
and protest, like Kavanaugh's view of his outdated Church. It is
not a political statement on the present condition of the Roman
Catholic church, such as the *Slant Manifesto,* or Eagleton's *New
Left Church.* Because these are some of the books I have been
reading, I have surely absorbed much of these authors' ideas and
styles. But I mean this book to be a personal, existential statement of what I see of priesthood and Church at the present moment; I hope to relate this statement to the insights I have
gained from the psychologists and sociologists, and philosophers
and mathematicians, the social planners and social change
agents whose books I have read, and, in many cases, whose
friendship I have enjoyed.

To define a book in terms of insight rather than of scientific
research or of academic scholarship may need some explaining.
Insight suggests a view from the inside and a search for deeper
meaning. Erikson, in a preface to his *Insight and Responsibility,*
puts it this way:

> The level of discourse in these lectures is called insight. This is a
> form of discernment hard to define and harder to defend, for it in-
> cludes those preconscious assumptions which both precede and fol-
> low proven knowledge and formulated theory, and it includes en-
> lightened common sense and informed partisanship. Without all
> these, the clinician can neither heal nor teach; while he often comes
> face to face with his insights only in the act of interpreting, advis-
> ing, or, indeed, lecturing. By then, however, he may find himself
> formulating conceptions which must again be verified in systematic
> observation. Thus responsibility always renews itself. If finding ex-
> pression for such insights is one of the speaking clinician's tasks,
> and the building of theory another, then this book, by its nature,
> goes to the limit of the first task, and will be found wanting in the
> second.[1]

[1] Erik H. Erikson, *Insight and Responsibility* (New York: Norton, 1964),
p. 10.

Those who prefer research findings to insight, will find much to interest them in Fichter's *Religion as an Occupation,* and in his *Priest and People.* Sister Marie Augusta Neal's *Values and Interests in Social Change* contains a perceptive study of attitudes to change among priests. However, for the purpose of this book, these competent studies have limited value; the wider view and the long time perspective which our insight covers is very different from the scientifically limited view of the research worker and statistician. The present limitations of social research—the difficulty of securing adequate sampling, the large number of subjects who refuse to answer letters, to fill in questionnaires, or whose emotional reactions tend to skew an interview, the difficulty of making deeper human reactions measurable for statistical purposes—all of these factors limit the value of social research for the kind of book this aims to be. Where possible, the findings of relevant research will be referred to, and throughout I have tried to use what studies are available as a check on the opinions, observations and insights I have considered. The two styles of study and consideration seem to be mutually fruitful, sometimes complementary and sometimes in conflict.

An example of this difficulty occurred recently during a seminar for priests—we had been discussing the changing role of the priest, and some of the factors leading to a lessening in the former high status of the clergy. One of those present had with him Fichter's *Priest and People,* and suggested that this scientific study proved that the priest's social status was rising. Here, then, it was necessary to reemphasize that social status was not a simple, easily measurable concept but a rather complex one, and to explain that Fichter had treated this complexity in a full chapter of his earlier book, *Religion as an Occupation.* In *Priest and People* he had taken a well defined, small area for study. From a sample of 4,560 diocesan priests engaged in pastoral work, he had received a forty-seven percent response. This meant that his study was not of the average American priest, but of those who answered letters of this type. The lay people in the study were provided by some 1,500 of his priest respondents who were prepared to distribute questionnaires to three "most active and cooperative adult Catholics." The lay people who cooperated formed the basis of the study. Fichter states clearly that they are not considered as a cross section of laity, but as friends of the parish clergy. When we use the word scientific about any social survey, we take all the inherent limitations of this type into account. This study of cooperative priests and their cooperative lay friends is useful and interesting, but it did not relate very clearly to the topic of our seminar, which was much more concerned with the reactions of priests as a whole in their relation to the parishioners not covered in Fichter's survey.

The complexity of the concept of social status is an example of the difficulty in writing a book of this type. So many of the concepts used in sociology and psychology are far from simple; further studies from time to time refine their meaning, subdivide them, and redefine them. In a scientific thesis one must take note of all this, to the point of tedium. In a book of this type, it is hardly desirable to go off on long tangents at the mention of words such as role, superego, group, community or identity. I can only use them in an accepted sense, and hope that this will not offend the learned reader. I can only hope, too, that my flights of insight will not too often contradict the findings of the research workers. If this should happen, it leaves the way open for further discussion, more perceptive insight, and, perhaps, further social research.

All study of this kind, whether based on research or on informed insight and experience, must necessarily be tentative and probing rather than conclusive and dogmatic. So very little reliable research has been done, and so few books of this type have as yet appeared that we are certainly at the beginning of a study of the priestly life in sociological and psychological terms rather than anywhere near the point of definite and final conclusions.

It is necessary to emphasize that, although this book deals with priests and with the present situation of the Roman Catholic church, it is in no real sense a religious book. It is not a theological work, much less a work of religious commentary; it makes no use of theological method. Its area is that of the psychology and sociology of the professions. It attempts a personal view, a view from within, using, as we have seen, an informed insight as its chief method and style. It makes use freely of some of the ideas, theories and research findings of psychology and sociology. Just as a book on the role change and identity confusion among high school teachers would necessarily have to explain, as it moves along, some of the theory and practice of schoolteaching, and might well be written by an experienced teacher, so this book will attempt to explain current professional problems of the Roman Catholic clergy from the view of my own experience and of current writing on these professional problems. In this way, I hope to be able to show these problems in the framework of a living, existential concern for the very real and likable human beings involved in them.

I must emphasize, too, that this book sees the priest in his social functioning. Priests who read it may feel that there is a good deal more to their priesthood than this book discusses. I would hope they do feel this way. While my aim is to study the priest as part of an evolving social reality and to describe this in terms of the social sciences, this process should help priests to distinguish more clearly their rapidly changing social function from the deeper and continuing meaning of priesthood which is too often obscured.

The Roman Catholic priest is, in our developed Western societies, a highly significant social functionary. A number of studies have revealed that when people are in trouble, they go in large proportions to their local clergy for initial guidance and support. Social workers and psychotherapists may be conscious of the ambiguity of this choice in many cases; however, along with possible negative elements of non-growth which we will examine in later chapters, there are often strongly positive elements of group identity and security involved in the choice of the priest as guide and support. The development of the role of the priest, and the tensions of adjustment he may be experiencing, become, therefore, important areas of social study.

The wide range of competent people who are concerned with social change in our societies should find much to interest them in this area. In the clergy they may see a large body of professional men who still enjoy public confidence and have a strong influence on public opinion. The crisis situation which this book will describe is largely centered around attitudes to change—not only change within the church institution, but also the more deeply relevant change going on in the wider community. This change in the forms, images and identities of our society is variously experienced; the reactions of individuals and of groups are equally various. This book provides a case history of the experience and reaction of one of the key groups in our ongoing social tradition.

1: WHO IS A PRIEST? /
a problem of group identity

Central to the growing up of every man is the question he puts to himself, "Who, really, am I—what do people see in me?" This inner search for a satisfying identity begins in early childhood, reaches a crisis point in adolescence, and continues on through the later high points of full adulthood, middle age and the approach to death. All of us face this identity question not only in relation to our inner self and its meaning, but also in relation to our lifework, our sexual identity, our occupation, our role in society. Crowding in to confuse our self search for an inner meaning come the questions, "Just what is the use of what I do? Am I wasting my time in life? Has my sort of life no value anymore?"

On many men these last questions do not bear very heavily. To a bricklayer or a carpenter, the possibility of prefabricated and prepackaged houses made of some plastic with a poly-unpronounceable name, erected cheaply with bolts and spanner, may forecast a disturbing change of job. He may see a threat to his livelihood, he may lament the good old days, but it may not provoke much deep inner crisis, for, likely enough, he is not deeply identified personally with what he does for a living. These same questions of the value of one's working role might be very different for a tribal medicine man in an emerging African community. As he sees his traditional roles being taken over by the medical doctor, the teacher and the civil servant, his sense of confusion and loss may be deeply personal, for his social role has been his whole life, and he has identified his deep inner self with the values his role enshrines.

The Roman Catholic priest in the United States, Canada, England, Australia or New Zealand may lie somewhere between our two examples. He may be somewhat like the carpenter or bricklayer; it depends on his life experience and his degree of social awareness. If his life is somewhat sheltered from the rising storms of social change, and if his view of society is largely limited by what he sees on the surface around his parish, he may not be deeply concerned; he may well feel that all the change of thinking, of personal attitudes, of social structures, is not likely to threaten his secure position and role very deeply. He may feel confident that he can make what minor adjustments are necessary from time to time. Moreover, if his role as priest is not identified strongly with his deep inner person, but is perceived rather as a job on the outside of his life, even major job adjustments can be absorbed fairly easily. In an extreme case, a priest's deep life concerns may center more around "the good life," with its friendships, personal comfort, music, golf and vacations, than around the priest role, which he may carry out in a faithful, though uncommitted fashion. Such a man may realize that the changes this book will discuss are interesting, even serious—but as long as they do not threaten his real life interests, he does not feel anxious or confused.

At the other end of the human continuum are the many priests who, from the viewpoint of psychology and sociology, are more like our African medicine man. They have identified very deeply with a traditional social role which has become the center of their life and attention, enshrining the main energy of their life dedication and purpose of living. The kind of questioning which this book will describe, and the increasing rejection of this traditional role by many of the thinking people of our societies, comes to these priests as a deep personal challenge throwing a question mark at the whole meaning of their lives, at their very identity as persons.

It is interesting to realize that this second group, so liable to deep disturbance, provides a picture of the ideal image of the priestly role. The ideal of the priest, both for the priest himself and for society generally, is precisely that of the man of deep inner dedication, absorbed in his priestly role, displaying great detachment in regard to other interests and concerns. Distinct from this image ideal, the social expectation of the priest would accept a good deal of compromise and balance between the life style of the "dedicated priest" and the "worldly priest" described above. Perhaps this expectation corresponds to a large middle group of priests who are somewhat dedicated men, absorbed in their role as priests, but still largely concerned with friendships, pleasures and comforts which do not seem too incompatible with the priestly image. These concerns may take up a good deal of their life energy. These men may be strongly self-critical, sensing a lack of integration between the ideal of the priest and the hard reality of their life of limited commitment. This inconsistency and the feelings of anxiety and guilt which it typically generates tend to blur perception of the priest's changing social role, which is rather uneasily sensed than clearly seen.

Here, then, is a group of men in our changing society who are subject to a large measure of occupational pressure. As they pass through full adulthood, middle age and old age, they must make satisfying adjustments to the identity problems and crises of these life periods, in common with their fellowmen. Because their chosen profession is peculiarly subject to the factors of change operating in our society, they must also make personal and group adjustments to a new and developing life ideal and role image. Whatever their degree of inner commitment to the priest ideal, their personal value system and life orientation is being challenged.

This challenge from a rapidly changing society is shared by

all the traditional professions to some extent. This is brought out by Erik Erikson, in his study of the problems of identity:

> the technological and economic developments of our day encroach upon all traditional group identities and solidarities such as may have developed in agrarian, feudal, patrician, or mercantile ideologies. As has been shown by many writers, such over-all development seems to result in a loss of a sense of cosmic wholeness, of providential planfulness, and of heavenly sanction. . . .[1]

The deep and rapid changes in our society reveal themselves in the increasing science orientation of our way of life and in the development of automation and cybernetics, with all the consequences of job mobility and the loosening of traditional social structures. All of this tends to create a general impression that nothing is very settled or permanent, nothing too sacred to undergo change and evolution.

This challenges the priesthood even more than it does the other traditional professions. As we have seen, the priest is ideally the most deeply involved of professionals in that he has an inner personal identification with the ideal values of his lifework. Because his area of interest is man himself and his deeper meaning of life and destiny, the effects of modern change on the very self concept of man in our society has an explosive effect on the priest's life commitment.

Erikson, in the quotation above, refers to the group identities and solidarities that are typical of different types of human society such as the agrarian, feudal, patrician and mercantile. But it is not only the group identities and traditional roles which vary in different types of society, it is man's own view of himself. Not only are his immediate aims different, but also his life view, his vision of reality, and his view of himself as a functioning part of reality. The work of the social anthropologists of our day gives us an increasing insight into the typical self view of men in, for

[1] Erik H. Erikson, *Identity and the Life Cycle* (New York: International Universities Press, 1959), p. 158.

example, a hunting society with an animist reality vision. In comparison those who live in a feudal society with an emerging mastery of nature will see themselves very differently. Instead of viewing their life and destiny as part of the whole natural process of birth, growth and death, in the light of an animist philosophy-theology, they will see themselves apart from the rest of nature, but tightly bound into the particular part of the fixed society of men into which they were born. They will see the shape of this feudal society as God-ordained, and their own functioning niche as "the will of God," as their own proper station in life.

To be a priest is to be at the heart of a social group. His role is to be the guardian and interpreter of the accepted life view and its attendant legends, mythologies and salvation history. The common self view of man within the priest's society is the base of his role, the background of his life dedication. As this self view changes in response to economic, technological, political and educational change, so the priest is faced with the challenge of adaptation or social uselessness.

It is a commonplace of social history that such a change in the self view of Western man has been taking place, particularly over the past five hundred years. There is every reason to believe that over the past fifty years we have been going through a period of greatly accelerated change. While, as we shall see in a later chapter, there have been significant developments in the priest role in the Roman Catholic church since the Middle Ages, it seems that there has been a notable lag in adaptation over the past fifty years. Indeed, the pace of social change in our societies, and of consequent evolution in man's picture of himself, his life aims and destiny, has been so rapid and far-reaching that it would be surprising if the Christian priesthood had kept pace.

It is possible, with hindsight, for us to trace the rapid changes of today back through the centuries, and this is a proper role for the social historian. One can show that our present technological revolution has origins in the mercantile revolution of the late Middle Ages, that it owes much to Albert the Great, to Bacon, to Descartes, and to the pure mathematicians of the eighteenth and nineteenth centuries; one can demonstrate the continuity of present change with the Industrial Revolution and the popular education movement, and so on. Useful as all this is for our understanding of man and his present-day meaning, we should not forget that it is hindsight, not the ongoing view of history as it was happening. Indeed, for ourselves at the moment, it gives us only a few clues for our future. The revolution in Western man's self view during this century is no less explosive because we can look back and see what led up to it.

During the years of this century, social change has shown itself in economics, technology, education and politics, as we have already seen. More basic are the roots of this change in the way man conceives of himself and his society. For example, Darwin set men thinking of themselves and of the reality around them in terms of evolutionary change. However outmoded some of his working concepts might now seem, the explosive force of his ideas has given a whole new direction to later thinkers and scientists, and has profoundly influenced Western man's view of himself as part of a process of evolutionary change. The whole process of individual maturing, of social progress, and of our search for identity and destiny is increasingly viewed within this set of ideas, as can be seen by the serious attention now being given to thinkers as widely apart as Teilhard de Chardin, Erikson, Harvey Cox and Alinsky.

Perhaps the most striking influence on man's self concept was that of Freud, who, filled with the contemporary images of physics, economics and scientific evolution, used these images to construct a new view of man's inner self. Taking these images of energy, of conflict, of evolutionary process, he gave us a dynamic concept of ourselves to displace the largely static self view of our forefathers. Although the neo-freudians, like the neo-darwinians and the neo-marxists, have refined, corrected and improved his theories, and the Jungians, the Adlerians, the Rogerians and the Behaviorists have added their share of disagreement, caution, praise and disbelief, Freud's fundamental insights into man have become a stable base of our Western self view.

This base, like all those that we are looking at, is a staging point; it is like the base of a climber on Mount Everest. It may be a temporary camp for further exploration, or it may prove to be a wrong location that leads to a cul-de-sac. It may be that Freud's picture of man is to be superseded by a picture provided by the cyberneticists or the biochemists. Still, this is where we are at the moment, so we must point to the deep influence which Freud has had on the common image of Western man in our time. He himself saw how tentative were the conclusions of his lifework. Writing in old age a final summary of his theories, he stated:

> We shall not be disappointed, but on the contrary we shall find it entirely intelligible, if we are led to the conclusion that the final outcome of the struggle which we have engaged in depends on *quantitative* relations, upon the amount of energy which we can mobilize in the patient to our advantage, in comparison with the amount of energy of the forces working against us . . . we are here concerned with therapy only in so far as it works by psychological methods; and for the time being we have none other. The future may teach us how to exercise a direct influence, by means of particular chemical substances, upon the amounts of energy and their distribution in the apparatus of the mind. It may be that there are other undreamt-of possibilities of therapy. But for the moment we have nothing better at our disposal than the technique of psychoanalysis, and for that reason, in spite of its limitations, it is not to be despised.[2]

Sociology from the days of Weber and Durkheim on has been contributing its own dynamic picture of society in evolutionary process. And when the sociologists and the new psychologists meet in social psychology to consider what happens to man in

[2] Sigmund Freud, *An Outline of Psycho-analysis* (New York: Norton, 1949), p. 48.

this changing society and how this change affects him in his various family and social relationships, a further depth is given to our emerging image of ourselves. We have studied the influence of the small group, as well as that of the wider community, on our individual thinking and personal development; and so group dynamics is added to the field of the new humanities.

Historians have added their expertise to this whole trend of seeing man dynamically in his social relationships; social history has developed a style of showing us the ways in which the surface events of history, wars, revolutions, technological and economic developments, literary and educational movements, have affected ordinary men in their way and view of life. Social anthropology has been giving us further enrichment of the trend by studying minutely the differing types of societies remaining in the forgotten corners of the earth. Such scholars as Malinowski, Ruth Benedict, Margaret Mead and Peter Buck have demonstrated to us not only the wide variety of life styles and reality views current in the world today, but also how people and groups react to rapid evolutionary change.

Philosophy, which in former days reigned serenely as queen of the sciences and meditated quietly on the eternal verities of logic, epistemology and metaphysics, has reacted to the new reality view with a bewildering set of trends leading us into mathematical logic, linguistic analysis, existentialism and personalism. When we find that Carl Rogers is a student of Kierkegaard, that Erikson is influenced by Martin Buber, we begin to realize how deeply the newly breaking ideas on man and his life ways are entering into our studies, our practical skills, our very way of thinking.

Finally, Christian theology, recovering from its sterile period of inner conflict and polemic after the Reformation, inevitably has begun to study and make use of these new skills and trends. Beginning with a scientific view of scriptural studies, and a slowly growing attention to the skills of literary analysis, social history and anthropology, formal theology has begun to reconsider such areas as the development of doctrine, the changing nature of church community, personal encounter in the sacraments, and the revolutionary and developmental world view presented in the Old and New Testaments.

The way in which this ferment of new thinking has its effect is clear in the area of sexuality. Following on Freud's basic insight, modern man sees his sexuality as a central dynamism of his growth, his identity search and his interpersonal relationships. Each of the disciplines and trends outlined above adds its quota of meaning, often by way of conflict, to this basic insight. We see sexual growth and activity in terms of dynamic energy, life urge, the integrity growth of the person, group identity, and the growth value of warm-hearted interpersonal relationships. Situation ethics, personalist and existentialist philosophies, and a general sense that all the old values are changing, lead us to the present social confusion on sexual mores. It is no wonder that the traditional Christian positions on divorce, family planning, contraception, masturbation, premarital intercourse and homosexuality no longer seem quite so certain, clear and unchangeable. And the Catholic priest, the social guardian of the traditional morality, becomes increasingly uncertain; his professional training in this area of sexuality seems increasingly inadequate and irrelevant. While his own sexual identity as a dedicated celibate is itself under serious question and is the subject of an evolving legal reform, he watches the revolution in sexual mores happening around him, and wonders whether to study the hesitant pronouncements of the Vatican Council, the uncertain statements of Pope Paul VI, the latest speculations of Margaret Mead, or the confident flamboyance of Hefner in *Playboy* magazine.

Multiply this picture ten times over—since what is happening in the area of sexuality is symptomatic of a general condition—and we have a view of the wide confusion of ideas in which the priest is groping. All these areas, which we could spend many books discussing in detail, are key areas of the priest's personal life experience, of his self-meaning, of his social function and role. To this must be added the continuing effect of numbers of prominent priests resigning from their ministry; and for every one who is prominent enough to reach the headlines, there are ten whose effect is also great because they are friends and colleagues of so many priests, and near enough to be real people. We must also consider the effect of the thorough reform going on in seminaries; excellent as this might be as an attempt to train men for the Church of tomorrow with a new vision adapted to the needs of emerging societies, its whole effect on priests is one of adding further to their self-doubt and confusion. And, as the Koreans were said to have voted with their feet, the young Catholic men of today seem to be passing a massive vote of no confidence in the priesthood by staying away from even the new type seminaries, or by going to them for a few years and then leaving for other occupations.

The priests of today are men in crisis. For some of them the crisis is quite clearly seen; for most, it is rather uneasily sensed. The crisis is heightened by the fact that those who seem least perceptive of it are those of the "official Church." This may be quite understandable; bishops, chancery officials, curial officers in Rome and the Pope himself are normally removed by their formalized life style from the personal experience of trends and opinions which comes directly to the working priest. However, this lack of perceptiveness at the upper levels of church authority leaves the priests more than ever isolated in their crisis of identity and role, for they sense a growing gap between themselves and the authority structure of the Church.

This gap was recognized recently by Bishop Christopher Butler, one of the leading theorists of church reform during the Vatican Council. He was commenting on the decision of Charles Davis to resign his priesthood and to leave the institutional

Church, where he was highly regarded as a theologian of promise. Butler referred to a general surprise at the strong criticism still continuing within the Church following on the council, which had, after all, been so concerned with reform and adaptation. "It is possible," he stated:

> that only now, in our life-time, have Catholics felt able to voice their discontent without fear of immediate reprisals by authority. If this is the reason, it suggests that the trouble in the body ecclesiastic is far more deep-seated than it is comfortable—for those in authority—to contemplate . . . it is the young clergy and the intelligent laity who provide most of the criticism. Yet we must remember that the vocal critics have many silent and anxious sympathizers . . . the volume and quality of the criticisms, even when they are not accompanied by severance from the church, are a serious warning to ecclesiastical authorities.[3]

THE VATICAN COUNCIL AND PRIESTS

The Vatican Council was held between 1962 and 1965 as a supreme consulting and governing body of the Roman Catholic church. It was made up of the Pope and the bishops from all around the world. Priests were not invited to take part, except as experts assisting the bishops on various subjects, a role also carried out by lay people. Some few bishops, through questionnaires and seminars, discussed the affairs of the council with their priests, but it seems that the majority of bishops did not involve their priests in any substantial discussions until after the documents were voted on and promulgated. This general lack of consultation was widely commented on by priests; they read with interest reports of the efforts of the few bishops who did discuss the council with their priests from the beginning. In fact, midway through the council the comment was being heard from Rome to New Zealand that priests were the forgotten men of the council. It had been suggested that the ministry of priests would be covered in a brief document, but in view of the pre-

3 Report in *New Zealand Tablet,* March 1, 1967, p. 13.

vailing feeling, it was decided to expand this to a full essay. In the final session of the council, a statement of about 8,000 words was passed as the _Decree on the Ministry and Life of Priests_. This essay on the modern priest is basically a theological study, integrating this area into the wider theology of the Church dealt with in other council documents. When it deals with the life of priests, as distinct from their ministry, it is rather idealistic and triumphal in tone. It fails almost totally to take note of the priest as a person in a rapidly changing society, with problems of personal identity and community role. A brief paragraph at the end of the document covers this area by stating:

> While contemplating the joys of priestly life, this council cannot overlook the difficulties which priests experience in the circumstances of contemporary life. For it realizes how deeply economic and social conditions and even the customs of men are being transformed, and how profoundly scales of value are being changed in the estimation of men. As a result, the ministers of the church and even, at times, the faithful themselves feel like strangers in this world, anxiously looking for appropriate ways and words with which to communicate with it. For the modern obstacles blocking faith, the seeming sterility of their past labors, and also the bitter loneliness they experience can lead them to the danger of becoming depressed in spirit.[4]

After this brief but clear recognition of a crisis situation, only the vaguest of general solutions are suggested . . . the goodness of the world . . . relying on the power of God . . . the brotherhood of priests . . . the fulfilment of God's plan only by degrees . . . trusting in God. These worn ideas, so close to pious platitudes, seem to serve only to convince the reader that the bishops did not really grasp the nature of the crisis they so briefly described.

This failure to grasp the experienced reality of crisis is typical of the kind of cultural lag which affects not only the Church but

---

4 _The Documents of Vatican II_, Walter M. Abbott, editor (New York: Guild, America and Association Presses, 1966) , pp. 574–575.

many other social institutions. It is a common experience to take part in an annual conference in which some organization discusses yesterday's problems in the language of the day before, and resolves the matter by setting up a subcommittee to report back next year. This phenomenon becomes tragic in our case, because the Church is, by definition, vitally concerned with social and personal change. Cultural lag was inevitable at the Vatican Council because of the lack of communication and dialog which marked the dealings of most bishops with their priests. This lag is noted by Philip Scharper, who gives examples from the history of Western societies, and goes on to speak of the Vatican Council: "in considering the Second Vatican Council in this light we must be forced to observe that in many ways the Council just completed has shaped and fashioned not a truly contemporary church, but what the church of the nineteenth century should have been but was not." [5]

LIVING IN TWO WORLDS

The priest is often described as a man of two worlds. People used to mean by this that the priest lived in a "spiritual world" as well as the everyday world of affairs. The modern priest no longer thinks in this duality, but he is likely to be trying to adjust himself to thinking and acting in two worlds which only rarely come into contact. One of these is his increasingly real world of science, economics, sociology, psychology, anthropology, professional education, politics and folk culture, which he sees as his society, his people, his mission, to be responded to in open dialog, with full honesty, and a brotherly sharing of decisions. The other is the ancient world of the institutional Church, with its encrusted social structures, its myth thinking, its vertical lines of authority complete with weapons of censorship, excommunication and demands of submission, its narrow theological dis-

[5] Philip Scharper, "Frontiers of Theology," in *Theology Digest*, Winter, 1966, p. 286.

putes and its slow acceptance of humanist and personalist values.

These two worlds of the modern priest seem to be drifting apart rather than coming together. The documents of the Vatican Council made attempts, here and there, to bring them into dialog with one another; these efforts found only small success. Perhaps the bishops of the council were living so fully in one of these worlds that they knew of the other mainly by reputation; most of their advisers were professional theologians from church university faculties, inhabitants of that same church world. The priest who reads the council documents can understand the language, for it is the vernacular of one of his worlds. But as he moves out into his other world and meets his fellowmen, he must speak a different language if he is to be listened to; he must adapt to a type of thinking in which the church world seems distant and irrelevant. His sense of the meaning of crisis is unresolved even when he meets the new type Christians who center their living and their commitment in the world of everyday reality, for he must deal with these people in the language of their new ideals and with the interpersonal attitudes of the humanism of our time.

It is no accident, then, that it is precisely in the forward moving priests, eager to be working out the human implications of the Vatican Council and to be serving men and Christians in the real issues and problems of our time, that we see the full effect of the personal crisis and uncertainty of role described in this chapter. I know of no adequate study of this problem, but my observation indicates that priests of this type seem more liable to crises involving their faith and confidence in the institutional Church. Many of them seem somewhat anxious, restless and uncertain in their work, striking and valuable as this often is. While they may meet with much public praise and admiration, quite often there has been a notable breakdown in communication with their bishop or church superior. My impression is that many of these men whom I have come to know and admire have, without realizing it, effectively resigned from the institutional Church and are living in a compromise state of mutual toleration with their superiors. They are men of intense personal dedication, and they tend to show in their way of life an involvement in the crises and problems of men which perfectly fits the ideals of the bishops at the council. Yet their very work, their intensity of commitment, their openness, honesty and outspokenness seem to lead them away from the Church rather than into it. It is not surprising that some of them take the final step of resigning formally from priestly life.

While these priests may be few in number, their influence is wide. There are large numbers of priests who, with more tolerance of institutional life, follow slowly in their footsteps and cautiously share their experience. I feel that there is a general movement of the clergy, at least in the English-speaking world, toward this general direction and orientation. That the whole of this trend and its associated problems generate further caution, warnings and admonitions from higher church officials, leading to further uncertainty among priests generally, is a typical symptom of institutional crisis.

2:BEING A MAN OF MANY FACES / the priest in a changing role

As the style of social research has matured, longitudinal studies have been showing interesting results. A group of children, for example, might be studied at an early age for their position on an intelligence scale, signs of social adjustment, indications of early delinquency, and significant factors in their family background. This identical group will then be the subject of a follow-up study at five-year periods as they pass through adolescence and early adulthood. A picture is gained of their process of development which is often revealing. Some of the accepted results of the former horizontal type research have been considerably modified as these developmental studies have matured.

Little statistical research has been carried out concerning priests and their occupational problems. As far as I can tell, nothing has been done that could be called developmental. This is to be a thinking book rather than a research study. Before research can be planned and organized, someone must think out loud about a problem, speculate rather provocatively, and jump to some tentative conclusions. And over and beyond the areas that can be covered by our present techniques of social research, there are many fields and dimensions that can be reached at present only by intuition. Apart from the evaluation of social research, there is great room, in an area such as this, for new opinions and conjectures leading hopefully to insights that can be tested by experience and later research. Although it is a pity that we have no longitudinal research on the changing role of the priest and the problems of this change, it is possible to simu- late such research by considering the general experience of a priest's life over the past thirty years, and by pointing to the role changes that are evident over this period.

I have been a priest some twenty-five years. My experience of the priest role goes back a further ten years or more, since I and my friends during adolescence had close personal and social con- tacts with priests. Moreover, a young man entering a profession is keenly aware of the role played by those already well estab- lished in the professional ranks; particularly in his early days in the profession, he works under their guidance and studies their attitudes and values. In this way I can claim some experience of the priest role over a period of some forty years or so. My per- sonal experience of role change in the Roman Catholic priest- hood over this period has been checked by the experience of other priests and lay people, and by the typical professional writings of each period.

STATUS OF THE HIGHLY EDUCATED PRIEST

It seems to me, looking back, that the priests of forty years ago were much more secure in their status and role than the priests of today. By the standards of those days, they were highly edu- cated, professional men. At a time when anyone who had more than a couple of years at high school was well educated, the priest, with his four years of high school and six years of semi- nary education, was one of a comparatively small group of men with superior education. Poorer people, who made up most of the priest's flock, had often an exaggerated reverence for learn- ing, and high hopes of education for their children. They had usually a closer contact with the priest than with other professional men, and came to view him not only as a religious leader but as a man of learning and social wisdom.

The priest's standard of education has remained relatively unchanged over these forty years, while the standards of general education in the community have risen rapidly. Nowadays, when a bachelor's degree is the normal mark of a good education, and graduate study is increasingly required for many of the community's normal roles, such as school teaching and social work, the priest is no longer outstanding in his learning. In fact, the university-trained man of today is inclined to consider the priest's education rather narrow and outdated. Today, even people of lower levels of education and income have contact with a wider range of professionally educated men and women, particularly through better medical and welfare services and because their children are better educated. No longer does the priest seem even to these people so eminent for his learning.

Catholic priests tend nowadays to seek a wider sphere of work than the narrow interests of a parochial group; they move increasingly in the wider community where the defects of their education become more evident both to themselves and to the people they meet. They become much more critical of their own education. As a result many seminaries are in the process of integrating their courses with neighboring universities, so that their students may gain the degrees needed to have a confident position in well educated society. These moves, overdue as they are, will not restore the status enjoyed by the priests I knew forty years ago. Their status as men of high learning no longer comes with ordination; with this change many of the social and religious roles of the priest have undergone profound modification.

THE PRIEST AS COMMUNITY COUNSELOR AND GUIDE

As a highly educated man, the priest of forty years ago played a social role as a resource person for his poorly educated parishioners. He was looked up to as a kind of community expert who would know what to do and whom to see in time of trouble or difficulty. Because his advice was free, he easily fitted the role of family counselor at a time when affluence was still unusual among Catholics. This function, moreover, easily meshed with his own concept of a pastoral role within a community of rising social expectations.

This aspect of the priest role has far from disappeared. The priest is, particularly in areas of poverty, still very much the poor man's lawyer, psychologist and counselor. However, this role has tended to disappear in areas of greater affluence. People who can afford the services of a trained professional, and have enough education to sense the value of such training, have a decreasing dependence on the priest as counselor and guide. This role change is well brought out by Daniel Callahan in his study of the American Catholic layman. Contrasting the present role of the clergy with their role prior to World War I, he states:

> The classic stereotype of that earlier role (but a well-attested one) is that of the priest as a charismatic, central figure in the lives of his immigrant charges. Not only did the priest minister to spiritual needs but he also guided social and economic progress. His opinions were respected, his education and knowledge praised, his community status exalted. This is hardly the case today. The Catholic priest is still the object of considerable devotion and affection; he is still a highly respected person among the majority of Catholics. But he is no longer considered better educated or particularly well equipped to provide the layman with enlightened advice on coping with the economic, political and social problems of daily life. Where once the priest was looked upon for wisdom on the whole gamut of life's problems, he is now expected only to provide guidance on the more narrowly "spiritual" problems. In church, the

priest is indispensable; outside of church, he is simply one more person with one more opinion. The cause of this change is readily apparent. The contemporary layman is a different person from his unlettered grandparents. Inexorably, the status of the priest has diminished in the eyes of many laymen—not only because the priest's role has become a narrower one but also because the layman himself, in his general life, has less need of his help.[1]

It is noteworthy, too, that the priest himself is likely to reject his former role as community counselor and guide as he becomes conscious of his professional limitations. He realizes that family and individual counseling, running a community advice bureau, giving psychological and vocational advice, and providing supportive therapy for the mentally disturbed are functions which require a kind of training, competence and professional standing which he generally does not enjoy. Courses in the new type seminaries introduce the students to these areas, but, being given by qualified professionals, they contain warnings against using a limited knowledge to usurp a professional function. The priest is today beginning to map out a new concept of his possible role as a community auxiliary in this area of advice and counseling, a role vastly different from that of the priests of my boyhood days.

THE PRIEST AS MARRIAGE COUNSELOR

It is especially in the field of marriage counseling and pre-marital guidance that a major change of role is evident. The Catholic priest of forty years ago had a clear monopoly in this area for Catholic people. In my early days as a priest, twenty years ago, the security of this role was only slightly disturbed, since community and professional services of marriage guidance and pre-marital education were still rare, and had little attraction for Catholics for a variety of reasons. Looking back, it seems odd that the celibate priest should ever have filled this role of

[1] Daniel Callahan, *The Mind of the Catholic Layman* (New York: Charles Scribner's Sons, 1963) , pp. 126–127.

marriage counseling and guidance. It seems to have been a natural evolution from his role as the ecclesiastical and social ratifier of the marriage bond. From this viewpoint, and from his role as general family confidant, the priest came to see the need of better preparation for marriage in terms of personal maturity and an understanding of the interpersonal factors involved in the sexual relationship. It seemed natural enough that the priest, as community expert and resource person, could fill this role which related so closely to the religious values which were his primary concern. In this way, the priest's role as family consultant was deepened with his increasing understanding of the ways in which the factors of maturity and interpersonal relationships affected the general happiness and stability of family life.

The social usefulness and comparative effectiveness of these guidance and counseling roles of the priest are not in question. The emphasis here is to point to the role evolution which has taken place, and is still under way. It is worth realizing, too, that this change in his working relationships with Catholic people was largely initiated and promoted by priests. The early building up of the Christian Family Movement, and its related Cana and pre-Cana services for married and engaged couples, was due very largely to the initiative of priests. These small group services and movements of the Catholic community gradually learnt the values of self-reliance, autonomy and group initiative. I well remember the anxiety of many priests when the Christian Family Movement discussion groups decided that the chaplain should be silent throughout their meetings, except for a brief five-minute talk. And the group seminars for engaged couples and for married couples, substantially initiated and organized by the priest in early days, are now largely in the hands of laymen who, again, ask the priest only for a short address on the religious aspects of marriage. The remainder of the program is usually in the care of mature married people, assisted by psychologists, marriage counselors and medical men. A similar evolution of role is seen in Catholic literature on marriage: mainly written by priests a generation ago, the best books and pamphlets are now being written by laymen. A priest would be thought outside his field today if he were to write the kind of marriage manual produced by priests in former days.

This example of role change in the life of Catholic priests is part of a picture of role evolution in our Western societies. This wider picture is studied by Paul Halmos, who refers to the way in which the traditional functions of the clergy in England have been absorbed by other professionals. "We cannot help being impressed," he comments, "by the promptness and thoroughness with which the various secular personal services have put themselves forward to act in lieu of the spiritual consultants and guides of former times." Comparing statistics for medical professionals with those of church workers over the first fifty years of this century, he notes that while there was an increase of forty-six percent in the number of people per church worker, there was a decrease of fifty-four percent in the number of people per medical or paramedical worker. While he does not take these figures as a direct indication of role change, he does point to various factors in the medical professional, and in the public image of him, which led to a counseling function:

> their relationship of trust with their patients has inevitably extended the opportunities of patients to use these technicians of the body as personal consultants and, indeed, through their dependence on these technicians in times of pain and mortal anguish they have got used to exacting from them the personal attention which they so much needed. At the same time, the discerning medical man has always known that many an illness of the body is mainly a sickness of the soul, and, therefore, the takeover of counseling by medicine was a natural and spontaneous continuation of an ancient practice.[2]

[2] Paul Halmos, *The Faith of the Counsellors* (New York: Schocken, 1966), pp. 31–34.

It is within this wider context of change that we have discussed in some detail the evolution in one sector of the role of the priest. This has been partly a conscious movement on the part of more forward thinking priests, partly a general yielding to forces of change operating in society and particularly within the Catholic community. This change in the priest's role in relation to marriage and the family is a vital example of the whole process of change in the priest's role and status which we have been considering. As in many other areas, the need which he moved in to meet a few generations ago is gradually disappearing. Despite his intrinsic limitations of personal experience, outlook and education, the priest was generally socially useful and valid in this role. At the same time, priests are for the most part accepting change graciously. I myself have experienced this change over the past twenty-five years and have actively promoted it. Nowadays, I am delighted to be able to refer people with marital problems to a community marriage counselor. And it is a commonplace for priests to urge young couples, when arranging their marriage, to take part in a seminar for engaged couples under either Catholic or general community auspices. However easily this is accepted, it is but one of many such changes of role which tend to have not merely a cumulative effect but an interrelating effect of dynamic proportions. One priest remarked to me, after taking part in a seminar which I led on this problem of role change, "So much change may be all for the good, but what is left for us to do now?"

THE PRIEST AS RELIGIOUS EXPERT

Looking to another example of this type of change, it seems to me that the priests of my boyhood were the acknowledged experts in Catholic circles on all matters concerning religion. Their status as learned men, and the lack of study by lay Catholics of theology, scripture, church history or canon law, left the priest in an undisputed position. In fact, it was one of the social maxims of my Catholic upbringing that "you must never contradict the priest." Whether it was on the meaning of some text of scripture, the latest complex problem of morality or ethics, "the Catholic view" on Franco, Mussolini, international banking, war reparations, or the rights of workers, "the priest is always right." Priests and bishops generally lived up to this image by keeping their disagreements in private and by avoiding public controversy with one another.

It was with more than a little uneasiness that, in my early days as a priest, my colleagues and I heard of "good Catholic laymen" daring to criticize some priest's views. I remember a group of priests being deeply concerned about a trade union organizer who, during a strike, dared publicly to contradict the "Catholic view" on industrial relationships. Most of the group felt that he should be publicly excommunicated. On another occasion about the same time, a Catholic professor of literature publicly disagreed with a priest's condemnation of Graham Greene's novels. He was ostracized by many priests, concerned not for his literary opinions, but for his "disloyalty to the Church."

Over the past twenty years or so, the laymen of the Catholic church have been moving steadily into an open discussion of church affairs and of the relatedness of Christian teaching to the topics of everyday concern. Callahan comments that those who are most critical of the clergy and most eager to enter into open discussion with them, are those best educated in current trends of theology and church life, and those most interested in transforming the Church into a more effective force in private and public life. "They are, in brief," he writes, "the people whose impact on the church in the years ahead is likely to be powerful and decisive; in great part, they represent the first flowering of the changes which have already taken place." [3] Re-

3 Callahan, *op. cit.*, p. 126.

ligious newspapers and magazines controlled and edited by lay-men, such as the *Catholic Herald* in England, and the *National Catholic Reporter* and *Commonweal* in the United States, have grown up to represent this attitude of critical and open discussion. Most Catholic journalism is still owned and controlled by bishops and religious orders, but there is a tendency even for these official and semi-official journals to come under professional lay editorship. No longer can a man's views on church life and policies be dismissed because he is "only a layman." Some of the papers still edited by priests are, despite their difficulties of official control, among the most effective in giving an opening to the new kind of active lay thought and expression; outstanding among these is *Zealandia*, a weekly from New Zealand. This trend of open and free discussion within the Church is an indicator of a new status for the priest, and of a marked change in his role as expert on church affairs.

In the area of theological study proper, so long the preserve of the priest, laymen have more recently made their mark. In the United States particularly, more and more universities are making graduate studies in theology available, not only, as formerly, for students for the ministry, but also for laymen who wish to specialize in this area. As this trend is being taken up by Catholic colleges and universities, more and more Catholic laymen are becoming qualified in the fields of theology, scripture and religious education. During 1966, I took part in a number of seminars in these fields while in the United States and found lay graduates taking an open and competent part in the discussions. The change in priestly role is very evident on such occasions. Twenty years ago, a priest had an expert status in all religious discussion; today, he will find himself lectured to not only by priests with special qualifications, but also by teaching brothers, nuns, Protestant ministers, Jewish scholars and Catholic laymen. In discussion, the priest will find that his position in the Church no longer gives him any preeminence in theology.

In fact, the priest on these scholarly occasions will often find his theological knowledge curiously outdated. Seminaries have generally been slow in absorbing new theological insights, whereas the theological departments in the universities are headed, on the whole, by scholars with a more contemporary outlook. If their departments are to be authentically part of a university, they must be prepared to discuss openly what is most challenging in modern theology and scripture research. Without the captive audience of the seminary teacher, the university professor must be prepared to make theology come alive for the mind of the modern university student, who claims a right to more searching inquiry and more open discussion than is allowed to students in most seminaries. As a result, the laymen, nuns and brothers who graduate in theology from the universities tend to be more vigorous than priests in discussion, more open in argument, and much better versed in the various schools of modern philosophy and theology. This is also true of those who have graduated from schools of religious education, philosophy or church history; their competence often presents a challenge to priests, whose studies in these areas have often been shallow and poorly directed. Add to these the increasing group of well educated Catholics, who by selective reading of theological books and journals and by taking part in conferences and seminars, have gained a mastery of recent theology which might easily outstrip that of their local clergy.

The clergy are finding, often to their shock and dismay, that they are masters of an eroded competence which seems increasingly irrelevant. In a recent discussion with priests I asked some of the middle-aged men to recall how much of their professional theological learning was still pertinent, still being discussed. One by one they reviewed their long years of study in various areas: scripture, the history of dogma, moral theology, canon law, liturgy, apologetics; and sadly concluded that little of it was now of much value. One of them remarked, "I've thrown away all the textbooks and notes that I had. When I was passing examinations in all these subjects it seemed that I was set for life, that none of this would ever change very much. Now I'm starting over again to catch on to the new-fangled theology of the Vatican Council, to read up on the death of God, the graveyard of the Church, religionless Christianity, the meaning of crisis, the Dead Sea scrolls, and the disappearing clergy—I don't know where we're going to end up."

All of this amounts to an evolving change of position within the Catholic church community. The priest's role as expert in theology and church policy is no longer guaranteed to him with his ordination, but must be earned in open competition with other members of the Church. This aspect of role change is one of the most basic and important of those we have discussed, since it affects the priest deeply in his professional identity, and in the teaching and preaching roles which are primary to this identity. Obviously this gradual role change proceeds unevenly in different areas; it would be further ahead in London, Boston or Chicago, with their large intellectual communities, than in a rural area of Canada or New Zealand. However, the feeling of this change is in the minds of all intellectually minded priests. The serious and competent writings of such people as Gabriel Moran, Leslie Dewart, Michael Novak, Daniel Callahan and Mary Perkins Ryan are being read by such priests wherever English is spoken, and these writings are themselves a sufficient pointer to the kind of change in process.

THE PRIEST AS ADMINISTRATOR

Looking back once more at the kind of priest I was twenty-five years ago, and to my older colleagues of that time, I recall that one of our clearly defined roles was that of "being in charge of a parish." Whether directly as pastor, or indirectly as assistant, we "ran the parish," benevolently, I hope, but with no doubt in our minds as to who was in charge of the whole operation. There was quite a pride in doing this efficiently; a priest gained the professional respect of his colleagues and of his superiors by his administrative ability. Most of his people, too, respected him for his capacity to organize his parish. He was expected to take quick and effective action about a wide range of affairs, such as the buying of property, repairing the school roof, scheduling church services, preparing statements of accounts, answering problems in theology, settling behavior problems in the school, or the organizing of a working session or a parish money-raising drive. The more directly religious aspects of a Catholic priest's life in those days were, theoretically, much more important in everyone's estimation, but the "practical" side of parish administration and organization became the primary factor in the gaining of public and professional respect, and in the self-image and self-esteem which is primary to every social role. This, too, was generally the primary factor in the promotion of priests to the important city pastorates, and to the rank of monsignor or bishop.

The pastor of today in our Western societies is likely to see himself very differently. There is a marked process of role change evident in this area. There are, indeed, many pastors who would fit the picture outlined above, but their number is decreasing rapidly, and already they are regarded by their colleagues, their parishioners and their superiors, as being somewhat outdated. The modern pastor tends to use professional services where these are available. He will employ a parish secretary or business manager to see to a whole host of everyday practicalities. He may hire professional fund raisers to increase the standards of giving among his parishioners, and a roofing consultant to see to that school roof. Some friendly accountant will balance his books for him; a local social worker will deal with the behavior problems in the school ground. Much of his responsibility will be shared by committees of parishioners. He may have a school committee, a finance committee, a liturgy committee, a buildings committee and a general parish council to coordinate all the committees and parish groups.

There were, indeed, committees of various kinds in the parishes of my boyhood, but they were distinctly advisory in character. The pastor was definitely in charge at all times; otherwise, he was regarded as somewhat of a failure, particularly by his colleagues, for "letting his committee get out of hand." In many cases, the committees were merely disguised working sessions, means of overcoming the perennial shortage of funds by volunteer labor. The willing men who painted the school roof would be dignified as a committee, but in "a well run parish" it would be the pastor who made all the real decisions.

Nowadays, the leading parishioners are more likely to be skilled workers, professional men or business executives. Not only are they able to pay for work to be done rather than enjoy the old-time working session, but in a wide range of practical matters of church life, they have a greater competence and experience than the pastor. They will work with him only as equals, and feel that they should have a share in the decision-making process. An interesting example of this development has occurred in my own diocese in New Zealand in the growth of parent-teacher organizations and school committees. Previously in our parochial schools these bodies were groups of parents who were happy to advise and assist the pastor and the teachers. A few years ago, after a good deal of experiment and discussion, a model constitution was adopted for our parochial schools which gives the elected representatives of the parents equal status with the pastor and head teacher. The constitution outlines the different roles of the parents' committee, the teachers and the priests, and sees them working in cooperation on matters of school policy and fund-raising. Each of the three parties has equal right to call for independent arbitration in case of differences of opinion that do not yield to discussion. Once matters of overall policy and budgeting are settled at an initial meeting each year, the teacher settles down to teach, the parents provide the practical management of the school and its finances, and the pastor sees to the religious welfare of the children. This model constitution has been in operation now for some years, and the pastors, after some initial hesitation and confusion, have come to accept it as a successful expression of their new relationship with lay people.

This new relationship of priests and people is marked by a sense of brotherly cooperation, and a mutual recognition of their respective roles; the emphasis is on their equality as persons and on freedom of initiative in church affairs. This is well described in the *Decree on the Apostolate of the Laity* of the Vatican Council: "The laity should accustom themselves to working in the parish in close union with their priests, bringing to the church community their own and the world's problems as well as questions concerning human salvation, all of which should be examined and resolved by common deliberation." And the *Decree on the Ministry and Life of Priests* states, in complementary fashion:

> Priests must sincerely acknowledge and promote the dignity of the laity and the role which is proper to them in the mission of the Church. They should scrupulously honor that just freedom which is due to everyone in this earthly city. They should listen to the laity willingly, consider their experience and competence in the different areas of human activity . . . priests should confidently entrust to the laity duties in the service of the Church, allowing them freedom and room for action. In fact, on suitable occasions, they should invite them to undertake works on their own initiative.[4]

WHERE DOES THE PRIEST STAND TODAY?

In our first chapter, we saw the Catholic priest searching for a secure identity and self-image in a rapidly changing society. Be-

[4] *The Documents of Vatican II*, edited by Walter Abbott (New York: Guild, America and Association Presses, 1966) , pp. 501, 552–553.

cause he is a vital person to society and a guardian of traditional values and mores, he suffers some degree of identity confusion as he struggles to adapt his self-image and life commitment to the needs of people in the grip of rapid social evolution. He wonders where he is as he lives in his two worlds: trying to be open to the new world of dynamic change, and trying to be faithful to the church world of traditional forms, images and language. If the matter rested here, the situation might be difficult, but not necessarily confusing or destructive. Many people, after all, must adjust themselves to living in relation to two conflicting systems of values and images; often both can be accepted, and can even coexist creatively. In the two worlds of the Catholic priest at the moment, however, there is more often a confused intermixing than a creative tension. His "real world" of urgent daily events and crises of sociology, psychology and popular culture reaches out into the new religious views of reality, while his "church world," through the Vatican Council, has entered an ambiguous phase of renewal and adaptation to bring its structures, images and language up-to-date without any loss of traditional values. For the priest, the man in the middle, this is confusing.

William Lynch comments on the confusions of the mentally ill by distinguishing them from the creative tensions and conflicts that can coexist in perfect clarity. He goes on:

> The different or added element in mental illness is confusion. And it always seems to involve an intermixing of things, a running into each other, that is destructive rather than creative. This confusion of the ill is no mere intellectual confusion, in which ideas are not quite straightened out. Their confusion is far more existential and painful than that. For their confusion occurs right at the center of their own identity and their own most basic feelings. It is as actual as one person getting inextricably entangled in the existence of another, to the point of the psychic loss of the self. . . . It is difficult to think of anything more conducive to despair and hopelessness than the deep and continuing confusion of the sick. How should they handle confusion? By doing something about it?

> By doing something about what? For in his confusion the sufferer cannot name the question, much less answer it.[5]

To see the pertinence of this quotation is not to suggest that priests are suffering from a group neurosis, but rather to suggest that there are destructive and unhealthy elements of confusion in their group situation at the present time which merit closer examination and discussion, and that "naming the question" is the first task.

The present chapter has begun this closer discussion by looking at the evolution in the status and role of the priest over the past forty years or so. We looked at the former high status of the priest as one of the small group of the highly educated in a stable society, and noticed the trend for parishioners to catch up with the priest and even surpass him in the educational and prestigious values of our mobile and evolving society. The effect of this is succinctly stated by Erikson: "Status expresses a different relativity in a more mobile society; it resembles an escalator more than a platform; it is a vehicle rather than a goal." [6]

We discussed the signs of role change in four key areas of the priest's life relating to his self-image and social identity: the priest in his role as general family resource person and guide; his role as marriage counselor; his role as religious expert and scholar for his people; and his role as administrator and organizer of the community of his parish. In all of these areas we noticed a traditional role in process of becoming redundant through rapid social change, and concluded that the lag in adaptation as the priest reaches out for new and pertinent roles may easily leave him with a sense of being rather superfluous and outdated.

This uneasy sense is further confused by what I have described elsewhere as a twofold resistance to social change:

> While we notice, often with deep anxiety, that the ways of people have changed since we were young, it is hard for us to admit that

[5] William F. Lynch, *Images of Hope* (New York: Mentor-Omega Books, 1966), p. 71.

[6] Erik H. Erikson, *Childhood and Society* (New York: Norton, 1950), p. 246.

this could be due to deep changes in psychological and social structures—we are much more likely to put it down to the perversities of
"the young people of to-day." Our second resistance is against the
suggestion that these changes in people and in society could be
changes for the better. It is as if we had a vested interest in the
ways of our youth, in the values of our upbringing and education,
in the society which we helped to make. When young people joy-
fully crusade against these ways and values, and assure us that the
bad old days are gone, we tend to take a defensive attitude. While
it is part of the function of older people to preserve ancient values,
we must not let this function blind us to the fact that deep changes
of the kind we have described are taking place in the individuals
and societies of the West, and that it is these changes which are
being reflected in the church's present renewal. Priests, whether
they admit it or not, whether they like it or not, are themselves part
of this process of change.[7]

Here we have been looking at the status of the priest as a di-
minishing one, and various of his roles as eroding or disappearing. To balance this view, it is necessary to emphasize again that
social status is a complex concept of many dimensions according
to the various roles played by a professional person and the various groups who respond to him. At the same time that the pro
cesses we have considered have been going on, other processes
seem to have been moving the priest in an opposite direction.
Our consideration has been mainly confined to the priest in relation to the Catholic community. Fichter points out that the
upward social mobility of the whole Catholic group has involved the priest in an increase of status as the functionary of
this group. In a chapter titled "Shifting Social Status," he documents the factors relevant to this upward movement and concludes:

> The present social position of Catholics in America demonstrates
> that religion is only one of the criteria by which personal status and
> class status are determined. Catholics now possess a greater share of
> those items of value that are accepted as norms of status. They are
> moving upward in the social structure because they have a greater
> amount of education and wealth than ever before. Larger numbers
> of Catholics are now in the professional fields and in the occupa-

7 David P. O'Neill, *Priestly Celibacy and Maturity* (New York: Sheed and
Ward, 1965) , p. 167.

tions which carry prestige. Socially, they are moving vertically, and in the suburbs horizontally. They are now largely middle-class people in the large urban areas where the lower strata are being filled by migrant rural Protestants, both white and colored. Catholics are becoming more and more remote from their foreign ancestry, and this almost automatically makes them "more American." The point that we are making here is that the priests, seminarians, sisters and brothers of the Catholic Church also share in the general upward mobility of the American Catholics.[8]

Fichter also summarizes various studies that have been done on the family background of seminarians. He points to the fact that middle- and upper-class Catholic families provide more than their share of candidates for the priesthood,[9] and comments on the way that the candidate brings his social frame of reference with him into the priestly life. He points also to the time lag and the class lag in this kind of social movement; as a result, the lay people are always a stage ahead of the priests.[10] When we take these upward movements of general social status into account along with the various leveling factors we have seen operating within the Catholic community, we gain a rather diffuse picture of the developing status of the priest. The general direction of this development may be rather confused; the picture changes under our eyes as new priestly roles and new community structures add their own dynamism to the general situation. We may conclude only that there is a comparatively rapid process of social change, and point to the problems of personal and group identity which it seems to indicate.

Many priests may welcome these changes in role and status as a step forward. They may see the priest being gradually freed from the burden of many social roles which have obscured his true mission in the past. But even these priests are faced with the confusion of conflicting demands as they face the task of cre-

[8] Joseph H. Fichter, *Religion as an Occupation* (Notre Dame, Indiana: University of Notre Dame Press, 1961), pp. 117–118.
[9] *Ibid.*, p. 63.
[10] *Ibid.*, p. 87.

ating new roles while supporting what is still useful in the old, and of finding the style of life which will give self meaning to their commitment as modern servants of an ancient Church. Many other priests, perhaps the majority, will hardly admit to themselves the reality of this challenge and will be uneasy and confused as they make the least possible adaptations in their traditional role. Much of their energy will be consumed in lamenting the good days that are gone, and in worrying about the changes involved in the present slow pace of official renewal within the church community and structure.

3: CAN A PRIEST BE FREE? / the problem of initiative

The priest of today is the inheritor of a history which he did not choose. When he decided to be a priest, he probably saw himself as the bearer of a message of good news to men announced in the name of Christ, and as the celebrant of a ceremonial which would bring this message alive in the people of his church community. In most cases, he would be relatively unaware of the sociological dimensions of his role and of the way in which his personal perception of this role may have influenced his choice to be a priest. Aware or not in the beginning, he is now likely to be rather uneasily conscious of the effect of sociological evolution on his social role, on the style of his religious functioning, and on his self-image and identity as a modern man.

He reads of the trends of social change, and sees around him the effects of urbanization, automation, cybernetics and modern communications. He takes part in seminars to discuss organization men, the hidden persuaders, the secular city, existentialism, the new mathematics, personalism and the community of the future. He ponders over computers and self-steering systems, and meditates on man-machine interface. All of these point to strong social trends and energies which seem to have a mark of inevitability. His own freedom of movement is challenged, and his image of himself as a man who makes things happen comes under fire. His vision of social reality as a community under God, and of himself as the divinely accredited messenger, meaning-man and celebrant of this community becomes of doubtful relevance as he considers the forces of human history.

Tillich discusses the protest which existentialism makes against the system of industrial society, and goes on to say:

> Man is supposed to be the master of his world and of himself. But actually he has become a part of the reality he has created, an object among objects, a thing among things, a cog within a universal machine to which he must adapt himself in order not to be smashed by it . . . out of this predicament of man in the industrial society the experiences of emptiness and meaninglessness, of dehumanization and estrangement have resulted. Man has ceased to encounter reality as meaningful. Reality in its ordinary forms and structures does not speak to him any longer.[1]

Some priests deny to themselves this challenge to their freedom and their self-meaning, and devote themselves to the shrinking world of their ecclesiastical subculture. This world is still large enough and vocal enough to provide them with a busy role as long as they can close their eyes to what is happening in the world of men outside. The dangers of this adaptation are evident. It involves a withdrawal from reality, which can easily become neurotic, and puts a man under the strains and tensions of double-living. Under these strains and tensions, a man is open to all the false reality adaptations of which the psychologists speak, as well as to all kinds of behavioral inadequacies and inner doubts and confusions.

Other priests will, in varying degrees, attempt to meet with initiative the challenge of new social reality. Through a constant rethinking of their role, and a continuing attempt to be open to the changing meaning of modern society, they hope to be able to make the necessary adaptations freely. In doing this

[1] Paul Tillich, *Theology of Culture* (New York: Oxford University Press, 1959), p. 46.

they meet a double obstacle: the very inevitability of social change seems to leave them very little room for creative adaptation, and the bulk of the church community, both leaders and people, demands that they keep to the traditional role in the traditional way so that they will not disturb the security and comfort which the Church offers to those who need it.

This dilemma is described by Harvey Cox in discussing the way in which theologians and preachers may speak of the meaning of God to modern man. He tells us that the theologians and preachers:

> represent the victims both of historical change and of social differentiation. . . . Especially when they dress up and strut about occasionally in their vivid ecclesiastical regalia, clergymen give people a welcome sense of historical continuity, much like old soldiers in the dress uniforms of some forgotten war. Or clergy are perceived as the custodians of a particular in-group lore, and as such are usually granted an expansive deference in a culture which has been taught to be meticulously tolerant of the beliefs of others, however quaint. But this dual role of personification of the past and preserver of a subcultural ethos, a role clergymen play quite avidly, takes its toll when they speak of God. Because of the role they have been willing to play, when they use the word God it is heard in a certain way. It is heard, often with deference and usually with courtesy, as a word referring to the linchpin of the era of Christendom (past) or as the totem of one of the tribal sub-cultures (irrelevant). The only way clergy can ever change the way in which the word they use is perceived is to refuse to play the role of antiquarian and medicine man in which the society casts them, but this is difficult, because it is what they are paid for.[2]

A further obstacle to the priest's freedom and creativity in facing social change lies in the way that he perceives the Church which he serves. The Church can be seen as a fraternity of free men, working together in the spirit of the liberty and creativity won for men in the life and deeds of Christ. It is seen also as authoritarian, with a set message and teaching which all must accept. It has nonelected leaders and strong discipline complete

[2] Harvey Cox, *The Secular City* (New York: Macmillan, 1965) , p. 246.

with organs of censorship and various punishments for those who disturb its present order and security. As both these ways of perceiving the Church are weighted with strong intellectual and emotional values, both easily involve the priest in a "double-bind" situation, making for anxiety and identity confusion. Rokeach discusses the ways in which we tend to isolate elements of our belief system in a self-protective fashion, and gives various examples of this kind of "double-think" situation, which he describes as "the co-existence of logically contradictory beliefs within the belief system. This is the well-known psychoanalytic mechanism of compartmentalization. It is designed to satisfy the person's need to see himself as consistent." [3]

This tension between freedom and authority within the Church itself may be dealt with by the priest in any of a number of ways; as this is an area of central interest to our general theme, it will receive separate treatment in Chapter 5. The concern here is to point to the various ways in which the priest may experience unfreedom as coming from the sociological forces and trends surrounding him, and to pose the general question of how best can the priest see to his free development as a person living creatively. If the priest does not find the freedom to move creatively within the play of the trends and forces of social evolution and within the scope of the authority demands of his church community, it is difficult to see that he can be building any new role which will be meaningful to himself and to modern man.

THE MEANING OF FREEDOM

We use the word freedom in a variety of contexts. Folk singers use it to celebrate deliverance from slavery and to urge the abolition of all forms of oppression and discrimination. Politicians make speeches about freedom of religion, freedom from want,

[3] Milton Rokeach, *The Open and Closed Mind* (New York: Basic Books, 1960) , p. 36.

freedom from taxation. Academicians talk about academic freedom, reporters about freedom of the press, and clergymen about freedom from sin. All of them are describing and aiming at the optimum conditions of community and group life that will favor the personal growth, creativity and dignity of human beings. All are recognizing certain basic values of initiative, self-decision and integrity which are threatened by chronic and extreme need, by unfavorable discrimination on grounds of color, religion or economic class, by limitation of the free flow of honest opinion, and by physical, economic and emotional coercion.

If men are to escape a sense of life-failure and a feeling of nonbeing, they must experience life in terms of a basic opportunity to grow and to be themselves. They must feel that it is within their power to aim at their full capacity in terms of personal satisfaction, inner joy and the recognition by others of their unique value as persons. Their achievement may well be limited by inner disharmony and confusion and by the force of outside circumstances. However, if the basic conditions of freedom are present, further personal decisions towards the achieving of their life-aims will seem to be feasible and worthwhile. In spite of the seeming inevitability of social forces and trends, a man will feel room to move within, or even against, these trends. He will feel that his influence on his own life, and on the lives of others, can be formative and creative.

He may well feel that he lacks the inner strength and integrity to make full use of his freedom, but at least the possibility is open to him and is basically a matter of his own decision and effort. He realizes, when he experiences the conditions of freedom, that he is able to search within himself for the values and motivation for the serious decisions of life. He is able to feel that his own truth and authenticity as a person might be discovered within himself. It is, ideally, from this self-discovery that we may learn freely to relate to others in terms of responsibility, respect, friendship and love; we recognize in others what we have discovered in ourselves, and from our inner sense of integrity and self-value are able spontaneously to say "yes" to the meaning and value of another person, or of a community of persons. We come freely in this way to value the common experience of a group or of the larger community, and to feel involved in their demand for order and law.

Most people do not verbalize their experience of freedom in this way, but they do have a strong feeling of the basic importance of freedom for their own meaning and value and for their life in a group or community. They easily recognize, too, that friendship and love must be freely given, and cannot be forced; in this way they relate the central value experience of their lives to freedom. The high value given by the folk singers of our time to freedom is a reflection of a very deep human experience which flows from our sense of being a real self, of being fully and authentically human, of being in command of the search for our own unique meaning.

This throws into high relief the importance of the experience of freedom for the priest as he faces the task of discovering an adapted status and role in the world of today. His role must be real and authentic to himself as a man of today, and it must be accepted as genuine by a generation which turns with enthusiasm towards the freedom of being fully human. The life task of the man of today is neatly summed up in the proverb: "I was born a human being—my task is being human." If the priest is to find himself as a meaning-man of the new society, it must be within the wide scope of free and mature human development.

THE FEAR OF BEING FREE

We have seen, in the beginning of this chapter, that the priest's freedom of social development seems to be hindered by the very inevitability of the rapid social changes to which he seeks to adapt his role, and that his dissonant experience of freedom and authority within the Church may also be felt as an obstacle. A further set of obstacles may be found within himself. He may well experience the common tendency to remain fixated at immature levels of submissiveness and dependency, and to sense the possibility of freedom as a threatening challenge.

It is common enough to find, among priests already confused by uncertainty of role, an apathetic acceptance of changes going on around them, and a tendency to cling to the security of "mother Church." These priests appear almost totally withdrawn from the reality of their social situation, as they bewail the evils of the times and exalt the security to be found in the least statement of the ecclesiastical hierarchy. These priests seem timid in their professional life, unwilling to take any initiative without permission of their church superiors. This regressive set of professional attitudes seems to be an uneasy personal adaptation to a deep sense of role-uncertainty and identity confusion, and takes its inevitable toll in terms of vague apathy and diffuse anxiety. While this picture may seem to be overdrawn, and to be describing an end product rather than a general situation, it does suggest vividly the feeling that many priests have been describing to me over the past few years both in personal counseling and in group discussions.

These withdrawal attitudes are, of course, not peculiar to priests, but are commonly met with when people are faced with disturbing challenges of close interpersonal love and of creative initiative. I have referred to this when writing of human maturity in terms of the demands of the marriage relationship:

> the danger of self-isolation is very obvious in marriage, since marriage of its nature calls for the most complete self-giving and receiving possible between two human beings. But isolation is a tragedy within marriage or any state of life. As we achieve some individual independence and self-meaning, we easily conclude that self-sufficiency is the final goal of life, and forget that we have won this

achievement of self only to be able to enter more freely and maturely into love. From babyhood on, we all suffer more or less acutely from negative urges which tend to isolate us from the love and warm-heartedness of others. Suspicion, mistrust, self-deception, anxiety, and our various false fronts always tend to pull us into ourselves, to cause us to withdraw into isolation.[4]

THE FREE CONSCIENCE

The internal obstacles to freedom and creative initiative in the priest can be seen from another viewpoint in terms of his maturity in the area of superego and conscience development. As a small child, he, like other children, would experience self-judgment and self-criticism in terms of his absorbing need to be loved and cared for, and of his instinctive reactions of anxiety about what may happen to him if he does what is forbidden. This level of self-judgment is described by Freud as the superego, and is seen in terms of introjection: the child making his own, in an instinctive way, the feeling and behavior demands of his parents. The resulting structure of self-judgment develops with us through life; it operates negatively at the level of unconscious demands, uneasy feelings and vaguely sensed anxieties, and positively in a general sense of well-being and self-acceptance. A second stage of self-judgment is described in Piaget's studies of the middle years of childhood; we see developing a moralistic stage of self-judgment containing many elements of magic and of primitive legalism. Actions are still judged primarily in terms of self-interest and of the type of scolding or punishment to be expected. It is not until the approach of adolescence that signs of mature conscience emerge, and actions can be judged in terms not only of what is done, but more deeply in terms of the intent behind them and the effect they have on interpersonal relationships of respect, friendship and love.

The early emphasis on sin, confession and divine punishment,

4 David P. O'Neill, *About Loving* (Dayton: Geo. A. Pflaum, Publisher, Inc., 1966), p. 86.

which has, until quite recently, marked the education of young Catholics, has had a confusing effect on this natural development of the child's self-judgment; in many cases, it has tended to inhibit the full development of mature conscience. In the case of young men aiming to be priests, the regime of seminaries, both at the high school and college levels, has been, on the whole, legalistic and authoritarian, with emphasis on keeping small rules, asking persmission for quite ordinary actions, and viewing life in rather moralistic terms. It seems to me that this whole educational development has inhibited the growth of fully mature consciences in large numbers of priests. They tend in consequence to lean heavily on the security of authoritarian structures within the Church, and to be emotionally incapable of creative initiative in their life and work. When they are asked to operate in terms of personal initiative and creative responsibility, they tend to experience unease and anxiety and to produce all kinds of reasons for doing nothing, at least until someone in authority has given them permission.

These internal mechanisms of defense add up to a fear of freedom and initiative in the priest. The attitudes of withdrawal, regression and anxiety which we have described are commonly experienced also as a strong urge to conformity. A man who isolates himself from the danger of deep interpersonal relationships and of creative initiative in his work will tend to compensate at a less threatening level by clinging close to his group in terms of a surface conformity. When presented with a personal challenge, his first question will be, "What are all the others going to do about this?" He will wait until he finds out what others are doing, and then follow the safe majority. Great numbers of priests seem to operate in this way; they show a deep fear of being thought different from the group of priests they know. They may even admire some priest who shows initiative in doing something new and unusual, but they themselves will stay steadily in the middle of the group, as if they were merging their personal identity in that of the group. This seems like an attempt to hide their real selves from sight, as if they were afraid of their true identity and authenticity as persons.

It is at this personal level that change must begin if the Catholic priests of today are to create for themselves a new and convincing role to serve a Church and human society in rapid evolution. Before we can go on to examine what general shape and direction their role might take, we must look at the personal development needed for priests, individually and as a whole group, if they are to move out with courage and creative initiative into the task of role development. There is some present danger that the changes which the modern world seems to demand of the Catholic church, and the tentative changes by the Church in initial response, will be experienced as a threat by priests rather than an opportunity. There is some evidence of this already in the numerous warnings and cautionary statements issuing from the Pope and various bishops since the close of the Vatican Council.

Our theme in this chapter has been to emphasize that the way in which priests are likely to experience change will be influenced almost equally by situational factors of general social change and by personal factors of the priest's own maturity, or lack of it. Rokeach, in his study of open and closed societies, stresses both of these factors and describes their influence on a person's system of belief and disbelief.

> We feel quite justified in concluding from the evidence presented thus far that to a large extent the shape of a person's belief-disbelief system is relatively enduring, "carried around" within his personality from one situation to another and accounting for many of the uniformities we can observe in his actions. But this does not mean that the situation itself cannot influence a person's behavior. Nor does it mean that a person's belief system is open or closed to the same degree at different times. We think of a person's belief system as possessing not only enduring properties, but also the property of expanding and contracting, or becoming more open, or more closed, in response to a specific situation in which the person

finds himself. We assume that the more threatening a situation is to a person, the more closed his belief system will tend to become. Just as threat or anxiety built into the personality as a result of early experiences can lead to closed systems that endure, so should situational threats lead to similar effects that should last at least as long as the person experiences threat.[5]

Rokeach and his associates made a study of the history of twelve general councils of the Catholic church in terms of the situational threat each council faced, and the degree of absolutism and punitiveness expressed in the council decrees, and found interesting evidence in favor of his assumption just quoted.

Priests are prone to this danger of closing up their belief systems in face of the threat of change. They should be conscious of the emotional reactions in favor of familiar security and against change which affect us all in differing degrees. They should look at change honestly and openly in order to see the creative possibilities it may offer to them. This will mean an effort to listen intently to those who speak and write about change in the Church and in society. It is useful to note the strong emphasis the Vatican Council placed on the priest's duty to be a good listener. This listening surely involves the priest not only in an attitude of personal attention to those who speak to him, but also in an attitude of personal attention to those who write about him and his problems.

Many observers have discussed the small proportion of priests who read journals which report favorably on changing conditions and roles in the Church, such as *Commonweal, Jubilee, National Catholic Reporter* and *Theology Digest*. Sister Marie Augusta Neal, in her study of attitudes to change among the Boston clergy, concluded: "An extensive survey of the reading habits of the sample reveals in general that reading orientation is conservative rather than liberal. . . . This general pattern

[5] Rokeach, *op. cit.*, p. 376.

indicates that the receptivity to change in the Boston area is not reinforced by general reading practices." [6]

Intellectual openness to the discussion of change must be matched by an emotional openness to persons and values involved in change. Sister Marie Augusta Neal suggested that those priests who saw life in terms of interest rather than values, and were not oriented to change, had a characteristic life-vision and outlook which prevented their acceptance of change, and presented change to them as vaguely dangerous. In the interviews she had with priests, she found in many of them a kind of emotional block which seemed to prevent them even listening to discussion of change. Most priests will recognize in this description a picture of a few priests they know well; it is much more difficult to see in it a picture of oneself.

PROFESSIONAL GROUPS FOR PRIESTS

A sign which hopefully points to an increasing tolerance of change is the rapid growth among priests of small professional discussion groups. In all the Western countries over the past few years there have been reports of the spontaneous formation of small groupings of priests to discuss their professional concerns in view of change in the Church. These groups can have an immensely liberating effect if they deal with problems which are really being experienced by priests, and if they are held in an atmosphere of creative openness and informality. In them, priests may easily come to be free for the moment from their professional image and from the formalized role-playing that often keeps their relationships with lay people at a level of impersonal unreality. Priests may come to be more open to the experience of themselves and of their emotional blocks, anxieties

6 Marie Augusta Neal, *Values and Interests in Social Change* (Englewood Cliffs, N.J.: Prentice-Hall, 1965) , pp. 64–65.

and frustrations. They may open themselves to a deeper experience of others and of the new realities of Church and society which are revealing themselves in our time. If a non-judgmental atmosphere is preserved in a group, the conditions for personal growth and liberation can easily be created.

Carl Rogers, in an essay on creativity, speaks of three conditions which I feel should be absorbed into the atmosphere of professional groups of priests as they reconsider their changing role. He speaks of being open to experience:

> the individual is aware of this existential moment as it is, thus being alive to many experiences which fall outside the usual categories . . . it means lack of rigidity and permeability of boundaries in concepts, beliefs, perceptions, and hypotheses. It means a tolerance for ambiguity where ambiguity exists. It means the ability to receive much conflicting information without forcing closure upon the situation.[7]

He speaks also of an internal locus of evaluation, indicating that the value of what we express is established not by the reaction of others, but more basically by the authentic feeling of being "me in action." We sense that "this is the real me, I am being genuinely myself." It is through this authenticity as experienced that we can begin truly to relate to others and to experience them as real persons. Rogers' third condition is an ability to toy with elements and concepts; he considers it probably less important than the other two. This is how he describes it:

> Associated with the openness and lack of rigidity described is the ability to play spontaneously with ideas, colors, shapes, relationships—to juggle elements into impossible juxtapositions, to shape wild hypotheses, to make the given problematic, to express the ridiculous, to translate from one form to another, to transform into improbable equivalents. It is from this spontaneous toying and exploration that there arises the hunch, the creative seeing of life in a new and significant way.[8]

---

7 Carl Rogers, *On Becoming a Person* (Boston: Houghton Mifflin Co., 1961), pp. 353–355.
8 *Loc. cit.*

Most of us can remember some peak experience of being part of a small group which came alive creatively and which, perhaps, had a lasting effect on our personality and role. It is good for us to recall the conditions under which this happened, and even to list them down on paper. As long as we keep in mind that this was a peak experience and cannot be artificially re-created at will, we may find that many of the conditions listed can serve to deepen for us the kind of group experience we have been discussing here. Priests who come to discuss the meaning of themselves and their lives in a changing community, and the shape of their future role in an evolving Church, which is itself relating to a changing reality, have a deep need for the experience of freedom which we have been considering. Otherwise, they may sense the inevitability of change as an impersonal threat to them, as taking from them the ability to respond personally and creatively to the challenge of living.

Their freedom, I suggest, will be viable if it develops in four closely related directions. It must be, first of all, reality-centered; it must keep close to the reality of situations, groups, persons and theories if it is to escape the tendency to be unreal, dreamlike and wish-fulfilling in a world of fantasy. The second direction is that of the person; by being person-centered, growth in freedom keeps its true direction of personal authenticity. It comes as a genuine growth of our real self, reaching forward into the maturity which frees us from childish dependencies and negations. Through this personal growth we come to see others as persons involved in the same tensions of growth and regression, and we begin to experience the freedom of creative interpersonal relationships. A third direction closely follows; our growth in freedom must be group-centered. It must lead us outwards from the security of our own life-meaning and from the warmth of a close friendship into the wider community of a group with its struggles and tensions, and its potential for a wider creativity. If we refuse to make this outward move, our growing freedom can easily regress to a sterile self-centeredness or to the mutual loneliness of two exclusive friends. Finally, our growth into freedom needs a fourth direction; it must be oriented to change. It must lead us to a tolerance of evolving concepts, forms, structures and people. Our demand that everything around us, including the people we meet and their ideas, should remain static and fixed for our benefit and security must be recognized for the immaturity that it is. Freedom cannot grow in an atmosphere of rigidity and attention to fixed forms; it challenges us to be flexible, tolerant, even easygoing in our acceptance of the changing reality of ourselves, people, things and ideas.

If these conditions and directions are not part of our growth in freedom, change will not be felt as an authentic experience of our inner self and its genuine meaning. It will be sensed rather as something outside us, perhaps threatening us, perhaps offering false hopes of a liberation which exists only in fantasy. Under the conditions of freedom which we have described in this chapter, a man can grow to experience himself as worthwhile and his evolving role as something chosen, creative and meaningful. He will come to see others as real persons, and where his life experience suggests changes in his chosen role, he will be able to share with his fellow professionals the task of role change. He will come confidently to see, as Rogers says, that "the facts are friendly." Whatever adjustments to his role and his belief system are demanded by a changing reality will be given an open welcome even when they bring with them insecurity and anxiety. The priest is committed to the truth by the very direction of his life; whatever reality the evidence of any kind suggests to him should be welcomed as a gift and a challenge. It is strange that learning should be thought of as something suited for children; really significant learning seems to be our most difficult task in adult life.

Maybe the most difficult learning for a man to achieve is the acceptance of conflict and contradiction. We find it hard to admit that we do not know all the answers, that we cannot yet find a satisfying synthesis of great and evident truths which seem to be at war with one another. We have been, in this chapter, looking at the inevitability of massive social trends and the inadequacy of the priest in facing social change; we have discussed also the experience of freedom as a working ideal into which we grow, something essential if we are to find meaning in life and work. I have suggested that we must accept the reality of both sides of this dichotomy, that, in fact, these truths need one another if they are not to be absolutized into meaningless dogmas. Harvey Cox, in discussing this problem, states that

> the issue is whether history, and particularly revolution, is something that happens to man or something that man does. Social determinists have battled with advocates of something called the "freedom of the individual" over this question for years. Is man the subject or the object of social change? The only convincing answer is that he is both, and efforts to sort out amounts of one or the other inevitably fail.[9]

However literate in sociology and social psychology a priest might be, he will understand modern society only as he recognizes that the very forces and energies of society that he measures are themselves a challenge to him to become more fully human, more authentic as a person. And the priest who thinks that he is fully the master of his little world can only find a genuine humanity in recognizing the fuller meaning of community with all its hidden forces of evolutionary change. Carl Rogers presents the challenge of freedom to those who have some scientific understanding of men and society:

> If we choose to utilize our scientific knowledge to free men, then it will demand that we live openly and frankly with the great paradox of the behavioral sciences. We will recognize that behavior, when examined scientifically, is surely best understood as determined by prior causation. This is the great fact of science. But re-

9 Cox, *op. cit.*, pp. 111–112.

sponsible personal choice, which is the most essential element in being a person, which is the core experience of psychotherapy, which exists prior to any scientific endeavour, is an equally prominent fact in our lives. We will have to live with the realization that to deny the reality of the experience of responsible personal choice is as stultifying, as closed-minded, as to deny the possibility of a behavioral science.[10]

10 Rogers, *op. cit.*, p. 400.

4: BEING A MAN IN A DILEMMA / *guardian of a changing morality*

One of the legends of my youth serves to remind us of the traditional role of the priest as a moral leader. The story is told of a learned university professor on vacation in the west of Ireland. His friends persuade him to come to Mass on Sunday in a little village church, and, rather reluctantly, he goes. They ask him afterwards what he thought of it all . . . "Well," he replies, "I felt it wasn't going to mean anything to me for a while, until that priest began to preach. He didn't seem to be very well educated, but he spoke with real authority, as if he knew what he was talking about. Things were right, or they were wrong. Things were holy, or they were evil. Oh, what I'd give to be able to have that kind of sure guidance for my life!" And the story ends, of course, with the professor sitting humbly at the feet of the simple pastor to learn all about right and wrong. This, like most legends, might really have happened some time. It certainly served, as legends do, to confirm the meaning that many people found in the priesthood in those days. Right and wrong, sin and holiness, heaven and hell, were perceived by most Catholics in terms of what the priest approved and what he condemned. He was regarded as the mouthpiece of a Church which did not make any mistakes in morals.

A changing world brings with it a changing morality and the challenge of confusion and non-meaning for the guardians of the old moral structure. A statement like this, challenging as it is to the theologian and the philosopher, is a truism to the social psychologist and the anthropologist. Piddington, a Pacific anthropologist, provides a neat description of the social functioning of religion in a recent essay on Malinowski. He describes the "integrative needs" of a community, including religion and magic, symbolism, art, ceremonial and organized recreation, and goes on to explain:

> Every human being lives in a community. He must share with other members of that community certain fundamental ideas about right and wrong, about the meaning and purpose of life. Usually, though not always, such values are held to be in conformity with the will of gods, ancestor spirits or other supernatural beings, and it is often believed that such beings will punish wrong-doers. Thus the rules governing respect for human life and property, marriage and family obligations and deference towards chiefs and elders are given a sacred character which is at least as important as any threat of human punishment. Morality becomes an essential part of the order of things, and the individual is given an assurance of the worthwhileness of his life.[1]

The priest, then, if he is not to resign from the ongoing reality of his society and become the old-fashioned guide of the elderly and the conservative, must enter fully into an understanding of the change of moral climate. As we saw in an earlier chapter, he will begin to see that rapid changes in technology, economics and communication lead inevitably to new images of the world, of the human community, and of the meaning of individual men and their growth. If the priest is able to be open to these changes and alert to the needs of people in change, he will be conscious that his moral teaching must be closely related to real life around him. If he is to be finding his new role as a priest, he must live in the real world and present to people a real Church.

[1] Ralph Piddington, *Malinowski and the Study of Man* (Wellington: Government Printer, 1965) , p. 16.

He must set aside any tendency to be preaching the moral doc-
trines of a mythical Church which does not exist anymore in
real life.

Particularly when he is dealing with children and adolescents,
the priest is subject to the temptation of the middle-aged and
elderly to relive their lives in the hopes and ideals which they
project onto the young. With a nostalgic yearning for what
might have been, older people tend to transfer the emotional
force of their life failures and anxieties into the moral teaching
they enforce on the adolescent. This may well be a particularly
strong tendency in those older people who have no children of
their own; their unexpressed yearnings for the kind of personal
immortality which parenthood can supply often leads them to
an idealistic and mythical view of the lives of young people.
Married people have often remarked to me that the religious
teachers in Catholic high schools might give a much more realistic moral formation to the students if they had children of their
own.

I have found, in discussions on new moral attitudes with
priests, that a good deal of their anxiety and confusion is related
to their unreal attitudes. I have often quoted to them a remark
made to me by a young college student: "Morality is for real!"
It can be very effective to couch some aspects of religious doctrine in story, legend and mythology, but morality is where religious attitudes meet the person's need for practical decision in a
real life situation, and it must be prepared to meet the demands
of everyday life and common language.

When we look at the values of our modern societies and of
what seems to lie beyond our evolving mores, we find a variety
of seemingly unrelated and conflicting trends. Many commentators have noted the technological values of Western societies and
the pragmatic, activist and instrumentalist bases of their common assumptions. With the opening up of the one—world human
community and the exploration of the vast and expanding uni-

verse, the insignificance of man and his absurdity comes to be an accepted feeling. It may be in reaction to this trend of thought and feeling that personalism and existentialism have come to be so important in philosophy, psychology and popular morality. Uniting with older humanist trends, they present the individual human being as a high value in himself; individual decision has a central value leading to the possibility of personal growth and the mutual accceptance of interpersonal love and friendship.

In this kind of thinking—at the philosophical level in literary work, and in folk morals—the individual human situation is seen to be unique, as unique as a person's fingerprints. Personal decision and commitment, the dignity and value of the individual, his unique opportunity for fulfilment, growth, love and acceptance, are seen as the operative factors of moral judgment. Personal conscience becomes much more important than universal statements of morality. Many who think deeply along these lines will inevitably find a place in their scheme of relationships for some elements of communal moral consent and universal validity. They will conclude that senseless cruelty to children, racial bigotry, and the denial of human rights are wrong all the time and everywhere. But the strong emphasis is no longer on any universal, essentialist morality which is, always and forever, part of a "natural law" or a "divine law." Modern man generally feels that he must think these things out for himself, without the help of gods, nature or priest. He has to see, in terms of all our expanding knowledge of man and community, what works in terms of personal meaning and growth: the warmth of interpersonal relationships and the mutual confirmation of person, value and identity in the human community. Above all, his thinking is tentative; he sees the use of only flexible values for an evolving society.

Faced by the challenge of highly personalist and situationist trends in the ethical theories and folk moralities of our time, the Roman Catholic church reacted strongly at first in defence of the unchangeable objective morality which was her recent tradition. Pope Pius XII discussed ethical existentialism in an address given in 1952; after describing actualist, individual and situationist trends, and current concern with the unique character of each human experience, he described it as "foreign to the faith and to Catholic principles." He continued:

> It will be asked how the moral law, which is universal, can be sufficient and even have binding force in an individual case, which, in the concrete, is always unique and "happens only once." It can be sufficient and binding, and it actually is, because precisely by reason of its universality, the moral law includes necessarily and "intentionally" all those particular cases in which its meaning is verified . . . the fundamental obligations of the moral law are based on the essence and the nature of man and on his essential relationships, and thus they have force wherever we find man.[2]

Various statements of this kind served to reinforce in priests their security as teachers of an unchangeable morality, based firmly on reason and natural law, and authentically interpreted by a divinely guided Church. However I recall, only a few years later, a priest-psychologist saying to me that tendencies were already evident within the Church which would call these unshakeable moral attitudes and priestly roles into severe doubt. We discussed the likely effect of new scholarship in the field of Scripture, and the insight it was providing on the personal mission of Christ and on the role he gave to his Church. We spoke of Paul Tillich's emphasis that Christ came to liberate man from law, not to impose one, and that man in his anxiety of conscience tends to create a narrow law of perfection for his security:

> Jesus Himself becomes for these perfectionists, puritans and moralists a teacher of the religious law putting upon us the heaviest of all burdens, the burden of *His* law. But this is the greatest possible distortion of the mind of Jesus . . . we are all permanently in danger of abusing Jesus by stating that he is the founder of a new religion, and the bringer of another, more refined, and more enslaving law. And so we see in all Christian churches the toiling and

[2] Maurice Quinlan, editor, *Guide for Living* (New York: McKay, 1958), pp. 215–216.

laboring of people who are called Christians, serious Christians, under innumerable laws which they cannot fulfil, from which they flee, to which they return, or which they replace with other laws. This is the yoke from which Jesus wants to liberate us.[3]

Tillich's viewpoint was startling in its implications for the role of the priest as guardian of Christian morality. Increasingly, over the years, we have found Catholic biblical scholars presenting the same emphasis. McKenzie, for example, has been strongly emphasizing that the Church is a community of love, not of law. He points out that Christ's abolition of law

> falls on the Old Law as a principle of righteousness and holiness. The believer does not have a complete code of conduct divinely revealed. He has no assurance from the observance of any such code that his relations with God are right. In a way which the Jew had never thought of doing, he must form his own moral decisions, for he has not a full list of "Thou shalt" and "Thou shalt not" to guide him. Both Jesus and Paul are explicit that the one commandment of the Christian is the commandment of love.[4]

Catholic commentators are emphasizing these days that Jesus came not to establish a new morality but to found a communal way of life based on personal relationships of love and friendship. His call to men is not in terms of doing or avoiding certain actions, but in highly personal terms: "Follow me . . . it is I who am the way, I am truth and life." He calls his followers not servants, but friends and brothers. He sums up all law and commandments by telling them to love. Consequent on this emphasis there is today a strong wave of criticism of all that is moralistic and legalistic in the life and teaching of the Church, and a great stressing of personal decision, commitment, responsible judgment and the primacy of conscience.

At the level of the Church's community life, the Vatican Council chose to highlight the picture of the Church as a pil-

3 Paul Tillich, *The Shaking of the Foundations* (New York: Charles Scribner's Sons, 1948) , pp. 98–99.
4 John L. McKenzie, S.J., "Key Words in Scripture——Law," in *Living Light,* Winter 1966–67, p. 96.

grim group, a people on the way, a people open to change. Here we see a community becoming more conscious of its human faults and failings, a community in continual need of reform and renewal. Nothing of the traditional objective, universalist morality is set aside—rather it is reaffirmed—but there is a striking emphasis on the value of modern psychology and sociology, and on the primacy of personal conscience. Freedom is stressed as uniquely personal: "the exercise of religion consists before all else in those internal, voluntary and free acts whereby man sets the course of his life directly towards God. No merely human power can either command or prohibit acts of this kind." [5]

In line with this rather ambiguous tendency, the Vatican Council presented no formal treatment of morality, but treated moral problems at times in a highly magisterial style, stressing the teaching authority of the Pope and bishops, and at times in terms of personalism and freedom of conscience. On what was generally regarded as the major moral challenge, that of overpopulation and family planning, the council seemed to recognize both streams of thought without offering any synthesis. After giving some recognition to the problem of world population,

> this Council exhorts all to beware against solutions contradicting the moral law, solutions which have been promoted publicly or privately, and sometimes actually imposed. For in view of the inalienable human right to marry and beget children, the question of how many children should be born belongs to the honest judgment of parents.[6]

It was announced that Pope Paul was forming a study group to advise him on this subject.

The moral role of the priest is confused by the ambiguity of such statements as these. This ambiguity was hardly dispelled

[5] *The Documents of Vatican II*, Walter M. Abbott, editor (New York: Guild, America and Association Presses, 1966) , p. 681.
[6] *Ibid.*, p. 302.

when Pope Paul, having received his expert report on family planning, still felt unable to make a substantial statement, but insisted that the matter was not to be considered as doubtful. Many theologians and commentators bluntly described this as a statement of the Pope's dilemma, and a flood of articles and television documentaries added to the confusion in the minds of priests. Lay people who had been taught all their lives to turn to the priest for the teaching of the Church on moral questions were now asking in vain for any sure guidance. This, more than any other single factor, has brought into explosive prominence the new and still uncertain role of the priest. This more than anything else has highlighted the confusion and role uncertainty of the clergy.

It is easy enough for us to understand intellectually that, after a long cultural lag, the Roman Catholic church is acquiring a new self-consciousness. It is seeing itself increasingly in terms of people, of persons and of their mutual relationships, and less in terms of an essentialist social philosophy and legal definitions. Seeing the Church as a pilgrim people, as the people of the way, as a community in constant renewal, lays a stress on movement, on evolution, on development, on a process of growth and maturation. The Church, in giving its tardy blessing to psychology, anthropology, sociology and social history, has absorbed into its own self-image the elements of process, growth and dynamic development basic to these modern disciplines. Meantime, most of the old working models of church life are still operative. Some are continuing on in an isolated fashion without much relation to the new trends, as, for example, most of the old discipline of censorship. But a great deal of what is traditional is now being quietly reinterpreted dynamically. A large part of the Church's working relationships are being revalued and recast in terms of the new images of fraternity, collegiality, human dignity, personal freedom and primacy of conscience, which the council, rather hesitantly, made its own. A good deal of this evolution is out in the open, as can be seen in the development of new social structures in the church community; senates and parish councils are evolving, discussions are being held more openly, public opinion is demonstrating its power to change the decisions of bishops, new rights of appeal are being studied, bishops here and there are being elected by priests and lay people. But there is another evolution which is largely hidden, partly because it is still tentative in its conclusions, partly because it is still too explosive in its implications for anyone to follow it through. I feel that the most challenging facet of this is the discussion on the meaning of sin; this discussion has a direct effect on the role of the priest.

WHAT DO WE MEAN BY SIN?

The concept of sin is radically central to religious experience. When a religious group is assimilating the basic values of an evolving morality, it is inevitable that the concept of sin, and the related experiences of religious guilt, repentance and confession will be deeply affected. Obviously change in these areas may have startling implications for the lifework and self-concept of the priest. We have already glanced at one basic development in the moral aspect of Christianity; it is coming to be presented as a non-morality. It is being seen as an ethical and religious ideal, a way of life rather than a system of morals. It is expressed in terms of a commitment to persons rather than a commitment to law and regulation.

The moral demand on the Christian is seen as a highly personal call from God to the human person, a challenging invitation of love which demands a "Yes" or "No." Many theologians are speaking of this human response to God as a basic or fundamental option, a life-direction; they see the life of grace as the dynamic development of our basic "Yes" to God's call, and sin as saying "No" to God in terms of a withdrawal from love, alienation, rejection of the positive values of personal growth and human relationships. Sin is perceived as a denial of the human community as symbolized in the Church as the community of new people in Christ. It is seen as a turning away from God, the symbol and source of love and interpersonal creative growth. From the viewpoint of child development, sin is presented as highly personal and relational, only rather ambiguously present in child experience.

The way in which this is being presented to children can be seen in the newer school texts for religious teaching. *The Australian Catechism,* a rather middle-of-the-way conservative text, states: "Saying 'No' to our heavenly Father means we do not want to belong to God's family. We prefer to march alone, without Christ, without God's life and love in us. It means we intend to do only what we want, not what God asks. This is sin." [7] I recall that, when I was a boy, we learned that "Sin is a deliberate offence against God by any thought, word, deed or omission against the law of God." The change of emphasis, over this forty-year period, from law to love, from the wrong thing done to the persons involved, from the individual to the community view, is evident in these two definitions for children. That this change is for the better is generally agreed; what is confusing and disturbing for the priest are the implications for his traditional role as moral guide, judge and confidential adviser. The custom of hearing confessions and forgiving sin is not only central to the priest's self-understanding, it is one of his striking claims which makes him different from other clergymen. Let us look at two practical questions in this area which are raised by the development we have seen in the concept of sin.

CAN WE REALLY KNOW SIN AND JUDGE IT?

When we see sin as part of an ongoing dialog with God in the deep center of the human person rather than as action or deci-

[7] *The Australian Catechism,* Book Four (Sydney: E. J. Dwyer, 1964) , p. 21.

sion against a clearly defined law, we enter into an area of ambiguity, of multiple interacting factors of determination, and of the unknowable. To a lesser extent, this is true of the judgments in the civil law courts. When a man is accused of murder, the various traditional formulas for determining legal responsibility are often inadequate, and expert psychiatric opinions are likely to differ widely. To a much greater degree is this ambiguity present when we ask ourselves the question, "Did this man commit a sin or not?" Even presuming the utmost frankness on the part of the delinquent, what priest is capable, in the few minutes at his disposal when giving advice or hearing a confession, of making an informed judgment of the basic life direction and growth stage of the person before him? Here is a precise moment within the development of the religious attitude of a human person, who is himself often incapable of making any intelligent analysis of his present religious condition.

Commenting on this question, Louis Monden, a Belgian theologian, discusses the relation between outer action and inner decision:

> If all that we have said about the relation between external action and internal free decision is true, it follows that although the external action has some connection with the inner decision which is its origin, it is very difficult to interpret that relation correctly. It is often asserted that the outer action is the sign of the inner decision. But the word sign might be somewhat too precise; a sign has a clear univocal relation to a signified reality. The outer human action, on the other hand, is so polyvalent as a sign that it might be better to call it the symptom of the inner decision. To yield its real meaning a symptom must always be seen within a totality of converging indications . . . masturbation may be the sign of an emerging sensuality not yet integrated within the total personality. But it may also be the manifestation of existential anxiety, or affective frustration, or helpless rebellion, or masochism. It is not an illness, but a symptom, as polyvalent as fever in a sick body.

He concludes that "as far as others are concerned, we can get to know hardly anything about the deeper ground of their actions. We are reduced to assuming, surmising, and guessing, and we shall consistently err if we consider only the outer facts." [8] In a way that is typical of the contradictions and compromises besetting the priestly role at present, Monden goes on, a few pages later, to discuss the priest's role in hearing confessions, and assures us:

> Both penitent and priest may be wrong in their judgment about the confessed sins; in fact they often are—much more often than our textbooks of moral theology suppose. If both are in good faith, this mistake does not matter at all, for God forgives not what has been confessed, but what has been signified by the confession.[9]

To me, this comes through as confusing double-talk. Monden tells us that the whole procedure of confession is based on an assumption of self-knowledge and knowledge of others at the deeply personal level, which is practically impossible in the circumstances; he then says we should go ahead and do it anyway, since it does not really matter. God is concerned with something different again, a meaning of which the accusation is only a sign, a meaning of which neither priest nor penitent may be conscious. Monden is regarded as one of the best theological writers on this subject; most of the others do not seem even to notice the question.

We should say clearly that, in view of all we now understand of the complex determination of human decision, activity and love relationship, it is now most difficult to make any judgment about the existence or meaning of sin in the life of a Christian. It seems that there must be a thorough reexamination of a good deal of Catholic practice, and a reappraisal of the priest's function in this central aspect of his role. This would obviously involve major research and studies. In the meantime, the question is hardly admitted into the open, and is having its effect all the more in terms of hidden anxieties and uncertainties. Priests who have studied in the fields of developmental and therapeutic

[8] Louis Monden, *Sin, Liberty and Law* (New York: Sheed and Ward, 1965), pp. 41–42.
[9] *Ibid.*, p. 47.

psychology seem generally to have come to a tentative compromise in terms of their two conflicting roles, largely by keeping
them well apart. Other priests, the vast majority, are left very
much in the dark. Many are discussing the reasons why personal confession seems to be attracting fewer people, and what
alternative ceremonies by way of group experience of repentance
might bring new meaning into this area of church life. It is unusual, in any of these discussions, to hear reference to the basic
question we have looked at here, or, indeed, to any of the several questions which confuse our consideration of the priest's
role as moral guide. One of the most revealing of these questions
is about the development of religious conscience in children.

DO CHILDREN COMMIT SIN?

Traditional Catholic practice works on a general assumption
that children become capable of committing sin about the age of
seven years. In medieval times, this was widely regarded as the
age of initial moral responsibility, and legal systems considered
a child capable of committing crime from this age on. There has
been a rather confused Catholic practice about the need for
children to go to confession to have their sins forgiven; the
widespread custom of beginning about the age of seven is comparatively recent. In most Western countries, Catholic children
from this age are considered to need regular confession, and,
particularly when they attend parochial schools, they are
strongly encouraged to go to confession, sometimes once a week,
more often once a month. From the priest's viewpoint, this provides a particular expression of his role which uses a good deal
of his time and patience, and leaves him with many doubts and
queries. Until recently, these were largely unexpressed—at least
in public—since they seemed disloyal to the accepted view and
law of the Church.

The arguments we considered above about the meaning of sin

and the difficulty of making any judgment about committing sin in any particular case apply with especial force in the case of children. But over and above this, a whole stream of thinking from child psychology has moved to bring the present Catholic practice into serious question.

Recent thinking about the development of conscience from childhood through to adulthood is dominated by three groups of psychologists: Freud and his followers for their concept of the superego; Piaget and his school for their patient research into the moral thought forms and images of middle childhood; and a whole group of personality psychologists for the light they have shown on the meaning of adolescence with its tasks, tensions and achievements, particularly in the area of personal and social identity and the growth towards mature interpersonal relationships.

1. THE PRE-RATIONAL LEVEL—THE SUPEREGO

As we saw above, the traditional understanding of childhood in our society always saw that the sense of right and wrong and its accompanying guilt feeling in the pre-school child was something different in quality from the moral consciousness of the child of seven or eight years. The small child was never considered capable of sin or crime; his actions would be described as naughty rather than sinful or criminal.

Freud's study of small children convinced him that, confronted by the behavior demands of their parents, children unconsciously took into their own mental structure a kind of mirror of the world around them, and that this new mental agency carried on from within a similar function to that of the commanding adults on the outside. It absorbed not only their explicit demands, but even their unconscious feelings and anxieties. He related this dynamism to the Oedipus myth, and to the child's dread of losing the love of his parents. This prerational function of self-judgment continues on through life in various forms; we experience it when we feel uneasily guilty about doing something which we know rationally is quite moral and proper. Freud points out:

> The superego continues to act the role of an external world towards the ego, although it has become part of the internal world. During the whole of a man's later life, it represents the influence of his childhood, of the care and education given to him by his parents, of his dependence on them . . . what is operating is not only the personal qualities of these parents but also everything that produced a determining effect on them themselves, the tastes and standards of the social class in which they live and the characteristics and traditions of the race from which they spring.[10]

This primary level of self-judgment is formed in the early days of childhood and is operating fully when the child comes to school age. It may express itself in conscious feelings, or remain partly or totally hidden from consciousness. Although for want of a better word I have called it self-judgment, this does not imply that it operates rationally; it is much nearer in style to what we call instinctive or instinctoid. The beginning of a primitive rational judgment of rightness and wrongness begins in the early school years, building very closely on the foundation of the superego, which, for some time, it resembles.

2. THE RATIONAL LEVEL—PRIMITIVE CONSCIENCE

Piaget's observations of the behavior of children in their middle childhood years, and his various tests of their reactions to moral situations, have been worked over and refined in numerous research studies. A picture has emerged of a kind of childhood reasoning about right and wrong, about praise and punishment, about fear and revenge, which is best described as primitive. This is particularly so in the early years of this period; as the

---

[10] Sigmund Freud, *An Outline of Psycho-analysis* (New York: Norton, 1949) , pp. 78–79.

child approaches preadolescence, there is a typical and well-marked progress.

The younger school child sees morality in terms of things and actions rather than of persons and intentions. Certain things are always wrong, even when they are done accidentally. The notion of God, when it is present, is seen not in the adult terms of the teacher, but in terms of childhood omnipotence, magic and revenge; it is a time, too, of sweeping disapprovals and prejudices. All of this can be typically true at this age, even though the pupil may be well able to repeat to the teacher the most sublime statements of Christian morality.

3. THE LEVEL OF INSIGHT—RELIGIOUS CONSCIENCE

Many child psychologists point to the gradual development through the years of preadolescence into early adolescence of a deepening moral insight. The child seems to see through the outward appearance of objective right and wrong into the personal meaning that actions and attitudes have for himself and for other persons. He becomes more aware of the moral importance of intention and deliberation. He is relating to other persons more maturely, is much more conscious of their personal value and dignity. His awareness of God loses some of the unreality of magical thought forms of earlier days, and he begins to see God in terms of tolerance, easy forgiveness and genuine love. It is no coincidence that these are the qualities he also hopes to find in his parents. He becomes capable of more insightful thinking and is interested more in the meaning behind outward realities.

Goldman, an English authority on the religious development of children, describes the progress of conscience in the child from about ten years on:

> Guilt is felt in relation to specific and concrete actions, not as a
> general condition, and, for the junior, God is still more interested

in vengeance than in love. The early secondary pupil shares this cruder idea, but is obviously dissatisfied and is on the borderline of recognizing that divine love and justice are compatible. Bad people, for example, are not seen as an undifferentiated whole and his group condemnations are beginning to be qualified. His view of evil is still very unrealistic . . . emotionally, there is still a very strong identification with belief in God, largely authoritarian in nature. But some confusions and doubts are already evident, even though they do not become frequently vocal until the end of the second year of secondary schooling.[11]

Goldman concludes from his tests a general age level of religious insight:

the stage of formal operations or propositional, hypothetical thinking does not appear to develop before a mental age of 13.5 for most pupils . . . this general age boundary coincides with the fairly constant indications from our material that religious insight generally begins to develop between twelve and thirteen years of age.[12]

4. THE LEVEL OF LOVING—CREATIVE ETHICS

It seems that the human person needs to build on successive bases of moral achievement in order to reach the full maturity of a well integrated ethical outlook. The instinctive feeling level represented by the superego, the primitive moralism and legalism of childhood, the dawning insight and personal sophistication of the adolescent; each in its turn gives way to a higher and more mature synthesis without really disappearing from its proper stratum of conscience. In those persons who reach a full maturity of human functioning, these earlier levels of self-judgment seem to find an integration and liberation in an adult attitude which has been receiving serious attention in some recent studies of personality psychology.

The way in which the maturity of adult living builds on the continuing achievements of earlier life stages is outlined in

[11] Ronald Goldman, *Readiness for Religion* (New York: Seabury Press, 1965) , pp. 134-5.
[12] *Ibid.,* p. 226.

Erikson's writings. In a notable lecture on the Golden Rule given at an Indian university a few years ago, he describes the moralist attitudes of childhood and the way in which the adolescent builds on them to search out the universal principles of human good and to take up an idealistic, ideological ethic. Describing the further stage of adult development, he states: "The true ethical sense of the young adult, finally, encompasses and goes beyond moral restraint and ideal vision, while insisting on concrete commitments to those intimate relationships and work associations by which man can hope to share a lifetime of productivity and competence." [13] He discusses the various forms of the Golden Rule in terms of the mutuality of trust and hope, the principle of active choice expressed in the prayer of St. Francis, and the description given by William James of the feeling of being "most deeply and intensely active and alive," of each person finding his "real me." [14] He adds his own concept of the mutuality which recognizes and confirms the uniqueness and identity of each person.

Carl Rogers, also, in his later writing, draws from his clinical experience to describe the ways in which his therapy has led some of his clients into a mature attitude based on an openness to feeling and experience, with a deeper acceptance of the reality of self and of others.

> The characteristic movement, I have said, is for the client to permit himself freely to be the changing, fluid process which he is. He moves also toward a friendly openness to what is going on within him—learning to listen sensitively to himself. This means that he is increasingly a harmony of complex sensings and reactions, rather than being the clarity and simplicity of rigidity. It means that as he moves toward acceptance of the "is-ness" of himself, he accepts others increasingly in the same listening, understanding way. He trusts and values the complex inner processes of himself, as they

13 Erik H. Erikson, *Insight and Responsibility* (New York: Norton, 1964), p. 226.
14 *Ibid.*, p. 233.

emerge toward expression. He is creatively realistic, and realistically creative.[15]

He goes on to comment on Kierkegaard's expression: "To be that self which one truly is."

Abraham Maslow is another psychologist who has absorbed a good deal of existentialist thinking into his personality theories. He has commented on the development of conscience through the superego and childhood levels to a condition of self-actualizing creativity marked by peak experiences felt as self-validating, good and wonderful, with an emotional flavor of awe, reverence, humility and surrender. Some aspect of reality, or the whole of it, is experienced with intensity in such a way that many dichotomies, polarities and conflicts are transcended, and the subject enters into a complete, loving, uncondemning, compassionate and perhaps amused acceptance of the world and the person.[16] Maslow likens this self-actualizing creativeness to the spontaneous and innocent freedom of happy children, particularly in its non-rubricizing effect and liberation from fear.

> The creativity of my subjects seemed to be an epiphenomenon of their greater wholeness and integration, which is what self-acceptance implies. The civil war within the average person between the forces of the inner depths and the forces of defense and control seems to have been resolved in my subjects and they are less split. As a consequence, more of themselves is available for use, for enjoyment and for creative purposes.[17]

It seems that these cross-fertilizations of personalism and existentialism with clinical and personality psychology lead us to a view of human maturity marked by a creative process of accepting fully oneself, other persons and the whole of reality in a dynamic interrelationship of active living and loving. A few years

[15] Carl R. Rogers, *On Becoming a Person* (Boston: Houghton Mifflin Co., 1961), p. 181.

[16] Summarised from the chapter, "Cognition of Being in the Peak-Experiences," in Abraham H. Maslow, *Toward a Psychology of Being* (Princeton: D. Van Nostrand Co., 1962).

[17] Abraham H. Maslow, *Toward a Psychology of Being* (Princeton: D. Van Nostrand Co., 1962), pp. 132–133.

ago, I described the full development of loving in human beings as an achievement typical of the later part of life:

> Only by continuing to love can we come to see—through and beyond the constant struggle to be loving persons, through and beyond the testing and the tensions, through and beyond the effort and hard work, through and beyond all the fun and joy of loving—that love is eventually our final acceptance of what is. We must come to accept fully the reality of ourselves, with our gifts, ideals, and failures, with our achievements and our faults. . . . We must accept, too, the full reality of others, seeing them as they are or hope to be . . . only late in life may we come to know love as helping the other person to be fully himself. In late life we may also trustfully accept the real world; we finally put away our daydreams and our castles in the air, perhaps even some of the stirring causes and slogans of earlier life. We must come to trust ourselves to the world of real existence.[18]

The authenticity of this picture of full ethical development seems to me to be established by its general agreement with the wise sayings of great men throughout the centuries. Christ was explicitly drawing on the ancient traditions of his people when he built a way of life around the loving of God, of one's neighbor, and oneself. He asked his questioner: "What is it that is written in the law? What is thy reading of it? And he answered, Thou shalt love the Lord thy God with the love of thy whole heart, and thy whole soul, and thy whole strength, and thy whole mind; and thy neighbour as thyself" (Luke 10:27). Paul was developing this old tradition when he offered to show his followers a better way of life, and wrote his eloquent hymn to love (1 Cor. 13). In it he told them that in this way of life nothing has any value unless it is done in love. John the apostle takes this thought a stage further when he confidently defines God in terms of loving without fear:

> No man has ever seen God; but if we love one another, then we have God dwelling in us. . . . God is love; he who dwells in love

18 David P. O'Neill, *About Loving* (Dayton: Geo. A. Pflaum, Publisher, Inc., 1966), p. 110.

dwells in God, and God in him. . . . Love has no room for fear; and indeed, love drives out fear when it is perfect love, since fear only serves for correction. The man who is still afraid has not yet reached the full measure of love (I John 4:12–18) .

This mature level of living carries its own built-in tension between love and law. However easily we accept theoretically all that we have discussed here, whether in the thought patterns of religion or of psychology—or of both—we still remain the inheritors of our own growth. Present within our lives, and often only partly assimilated into our higher synthesis of maturity, are both the positive and negative forces of our superego, of our childhood moralism, of our adolescent searchings. Our true self and our authentic life view may be present to us only in some peak experiences or in some moments of religious faith. The way in which these high moments achieve dominance in our lives and eliminate fear has been described by Tillich:

> It is not a new demand, a new doctrine, or new morals, but rather a new reality, a new being, and a new power of transforming life . . . suddenly we are grasped by a peace which is above reason, that is above our theoretical seeking for the true, and above our practical striving for the good. The true—namely, the truth of our life and of our existence—has grasped us. We know that *now*, in this moment, we are in the truth, in spite of all our ignorance about ourselves and our world. We have not become wiser and more understanding in any ordinary sense; we are still children in knowledge. But the truth of life is in us, with an illuminating certainty, uniting us with ourselves, giving us great and restful happiness. And the good, the ultimate good, which is not good for something else, but good in itself, has grasped us. We know that now, in this moment, we are in the good, in spite of all our weakness and evil, in spite of the fragmentary and distorted character of our self and the world. We have not become more moral or more saintly; we still belong to a world which is subject to evil and self-destruction. But the good of life is in us, uniting us with the good of everything, giving us the blessed experience of universal love.[19]

[19] Paul Tillich, *The Shaking of the Foundations* (New York: Charles Scribner's Sons, 1948) , pp. 99–100.

WHAT ARE THE ANSWERS?

When I look back over this brief sketch of the development of conscience, I am aware that the description of four levels or stages of growth in self-judgment becomes false in its effort to be clear. Life itself, and our human growing, is never as clear as this; it has no such clear-cut divisions, and its process is vital, not logical. This makes it the more difficult to give any sure answers to our questions.

Sin, as we have seen, is more properly a religious concept than a moral one; it supposes a personal faith in God, and a consciousness of belonging to the community of God's people. It indicates a deliberate deviation from a way of living by this faith and consciousness. It is a rejection of this communal life of faith and love, a breaking off, by some considered attitude or decision, of the personal and social relationship of religious commitment. "Saying no to God," then, is about as good a definition as we can achieve.

When we look at our second question, as to whether children commit sin, we must ask ourselves at what stage of their development do children commonly achieve such a personal relationship with God and his people that they begin to see their decisions and attitudes in terms of this personal and social relationship. Let us look at one outward action: Johnny becomes angry with his little brother, and, obviously meaning to hurt him as much as he can, hits him a cruel blow. If Johnny is four or five years of age, no one is likely to think that he has committed sin; a psychological explanation, rather than a theological or religious one, seems to cover his action. At the age of nine or ten, it seems to me that there is every reason to remain satisfied with psychology and common sense. It seems farfetched to presume in a child of ten a kind of religious insight into the deeper meaning of decision in terms of a personal relationship with

God and a social sense of being one of a religious community bound together by bonds of faith, love and common care. After all, if Johnny has a temper tantrum and tells his mother he hates her and will never speak to her again, she is not likely to take this as a real breaking off of their normal relationship of love and care. Even when we pursue our inquiry into adolescence, wise parents are normally very tolerant of the outbursts of disturbed teen-agers, and little inclined to take passionate statements, actions or decisions at their face value. Even if Johnny is still hitting his little brother occasionally, there may not be any real disturbance of their true brotherly relationship, much less the kind of religious decision that is the basis of sin.

It seems, then, that during the moralistic stage of middle childhood, there should be no more expectation of sin in the life of a child than there is in the earlier stage. The growing conscience becomes, in adolescence, more highly personal, insightful and idealistic; we must see here the possibility of the kind of relationship with God and sense of religious community which we have described. At the same time, we must give full value to the emotional disturbance of adolescence and be prepared to look below the surface of outward behavior for the authentic personal attitude. It is at this deeper level of adolescent experience that conscience may bring its self-accusation of sin before God. It is here, normally, that sin may first be experienced, not as a textbook concept, but as an authentic personal reality. In the light of this understanding, it is difficult to see how such a theologian as Monden can still favor the hearing of the confessions of small children. He states:

> Although the moral experience of the child remains largely implicit within instinctive taboo reactions, and although, as a consequence, religious instruction can be experienced only under a mythologized form and the practice of the sacraments only within a semi-magical state of mind, this is not a sufficient reason to refrain from speaking of sin, heaven and hell before the age of puberty or for putting off the first confession until that time. Both must be

adapted to the mental state of these years, so that the developing consciousness may rest on a solid foundation. It is very true that quite a number of people no longer go to confession later in life because in their childhood they experienced confession as a form of coercion, or as something frightening. This demonstrates that they learned in the wrong way to go to confession or that they had to approach the sacrament with an effective attitude which had already been thoroughly distorted.[20]

Again, this seems the kind of religious double-talk which leaves the priests in an unresolved role confusion. It admits openly the normal psychological description of the experience of children, speaking of instinctive taboo reactions and of religion being experienced under a mythologized form within a semi-magical state of mind. It admits also what clinical psychologists have been saying for so long about the sad effects of imposing adult religious values, guilt reactions and conscience forms on children; it speaks of confession for many children as frightening, as a form of coercion, and as resulting in an affective attitude which is thoroughly distorted. Then we are told that none of this is sufficient reason for refraining from speaking of sin and hell to children, or for postponing the practice of confession. I feel that this is typical of the resistance and confusion which beset the professional discussions of priests. A line of thought proceeds normally to the point where it threatens some custom or tradition of the Church; then there is a general withdrawal from discussing the logical conclusion, and tacit agreement on a confused compromise. Generally, this will be rationalized in terms of a better understanding of the present custom, a better working method, more education, more prayer, and so on. Because these are certain and admitted values, agreement on them is expected to clear away all doubt and role confusion. As we shall see in later chapters, the documents of the Vatican Council provide us with highly sophisticated examples of this kind of defensive thinking.

[20] Monden, *op. cit.*, p. 124.

A further source of confusion is a fairly widespread tendency to absolutize the new psychological insights which we have outlined, and to erect them into either a new and rigid system or into a new promise of paradise on earth. Some recent religious textbooks for children seem to systematize psychological insight and a developmental view of childhood to a point where freedom and spontaneity disappear. There are many people, too, who speak and write in an "if only" style: if only everyone would live spontaneously, or in existential freedom, or love to the full, or be fully human, or be self-actualizing, then our problems and conflicts would disappear; then there would be no war, no crime—and presumably—no hospitals or cemeteries. This is the same kind of thinking as that which suggested that if children said their prayers every night, or read the Bible regularly, they would have no problems. The three psychologists we have quoted, Erikson, Rogers and Maslow, have all had to emphasize that they do not offer any panacea for human problems, but that real maturity often sharpens our view of problems and conflicts precisely because we are open to the real world of existence and have got rid of so much that is unreal and defensive in our lives. We are faced with a greater demand of responsibility and of responsiveness as we progress to the higher levels of human existence which they tentatively outline.

WHERE DOES THE PRIEST STAND TODAY?

We have seen in this chapter that the priest's traditional role as a man of clear moral authority, the voice piece of a practically infallible moral system, has come into serious doubt. This doubt comes partly from outside, as a reflection of a changing moral climate in our societies as new images of the world, of persons, and of communities emerge. In this emerging world, people are ceasing to feel the relevance of a moral guide with fixed and ready answers culled from a store of unchangeable divine wisdom; they are asking the typical modern questions, "How well does this system work? Who, really, thought it up? Does it understand me as a real person? Does it give consideration to my particular needs? Does it get us anywhere?"

We saw that the Roman Catholic church is entering quickly into a belated dialog with the pragmatic, activist, personalist and existentialist values which these modern questions suggest. With this dialog going on, the Church is insisting strongly on the validity of its traditional natural law morality and its universalist, essentialist expressions. The priest experiences this ambiguity as an attack from within. Not only is the efficient and clever "outside world" rather sceptical of his traditional moral role, it seems that his own church community is in two minds about it.

Looking at one particular sector of this problem in more depth, we saw that the understanding of sin within the Church was in process of evolutionary change, and that a good deal of ambiguity and ambivalence had entered into this area, so clearly central to the moral role of the priest. Looking for more light on this topic, we saw something of the modern discussion of the development of conscience in children, and the theory of an epigenetic growth toward the maturity of adult conscience. We saw the recognition of humanist and existentialist values in the various descriptions of maturity, expressed in terms of being fully human, open to persons and to experience, becoming fully oneself. From this framework, we examined the concept of child sin, and the general Catholic practice of children confessing their sins to a priest. We saw that these were open to serious doubt, and that a further area of ambiguity and confusion is opening up. In many places already, parishes and dioceses are changing their customs and revising their moral view of childhood; in many places, too, priests are reporting a changed attitude to sin and confession on the part of adults.

It seems inevitable, then, that the moral role of the priest will tend to evolve at an accelerated rate. Caught in the ambiguities and confusions of modern society and the modern Church, the priest is left in a good deal of doubt as to where he stands. If he remains steadily faithful to the fixed values of his traditional role, his voice will be listened to less and less, particularly as it loses the strong, confident ring of former days. If he moves "way out" and fully embraces modern values and thought forms, he may well have an uneasy anxiety about his loyalty to his own church community which he lives to serve; he will seem to stand condemned by the cautions and warnings of church authority. Many modern-minded people within and outside the Church will be listening to him, but he himself may be going through the agonies and confusions of the uncertain revolutionary. Avoiding these unattractive positions, most priests opt for the middle, searching for workable compromises, and for the security of a united position. Here they find the ambiguities we have discussed and the anguish of the double bind where anything they do seems to be wrong in some way. They try to stay with their Church in its hesitating, partial reform, as it seems cautiously to hope that the whole process may not get out of control.

The dangers of caution and partial reform are evident enough. In public worship, for example, the Vatican Council decided on a cautious reform of liturgy, allowing part of the Mass to be said in the vernacular; what was not expected was the widespread view that this, in practice, was such an odd mixture that it made less sense than the quiet dignity of ancient Latin. A further compromise is now decided on, leaving the way open for all prayers in the vernacular, but making only minor changes in prayer forms and ceremonial. Experiments already carried out show that this serves only to highlight the need for further and deeper reform; ancient prayers which sounded quaintly archaic in Latin, tend to sound quite incongruous in modern English, and the accompanying medieval ceremonial seems even more irrelevant.

Priests on the moral issue are choosing their personal position. The practical moral problem of family planning has forced them to take up one of the three general positions we have outlined. None of these provide a satisfactory moral role for the priest of today, and priests look forward uneasily to the prospect of similar practical discussions on divorce, on abortion, on war and peace, on the practical issues of race problems, on the moral demands of wealth and hunger. There seems no knowing where the priest stands today, nor where he might be standing tomorrow.

5:BEING A PROMOTER OF FREEDOM / and an agent of authority

The modern priest prefers to see himself as reasonably liberal, as anything except an authoritarian person. He wants to be a leader rather than a manager. There are, as we shall see, many elements of confusion in this self-image, but the growing emphasis is plain. A firm welcome was given by priests to the Vatican Council declaration on religious liberty, which stated that "of its very nature, the exercise of religion consists before all else on those internal, voluntary and free acts whereby man sets the course of his life directly toward God. No merely human power can either command or prohibit acts of this kind." [1] This welcome was an indication of the way in which the modern priest sees himself no longer as a man of command, but as a leader who bears an invitation.

We have noted in preceding chapters the growing tendency to see the life of a Christian in terms of a call to personal decision, to grow in responsible maturity, to become fully human. This call takes the emphasis away from individualistic views of the Christian life, and sets it strongly in the direction of community

1 *The Documents of Vatican II*, Walter M. Abbott, editor (New York: Guild, America and Association Presses, 1966) , p. 681.

values and interpersonal relationships. The implications of this
trend are spelled out by Charles Davis:

> Life for a Christian in a secular society means a great stress on
> free, personal faith. He is no longer carried along by social en-
> vironment. That is the advantage of a secular society. It provides an
> occasion for purifying and strengthening Christian faith. It allows
> faith to assume its proper character as a free, personal commitment.
> But it would be equally a distortion of faith, if the individual be-
> liever were left in isolation. Hence the imperative necessity of form-
> ing primary groups among Christians. A primary group in the so-
> ciological sense is a group where the members personally know one
> another and are involved in an intimate, face-to-face association and
> cooperation. When Church and society coincided, there was little
> need for concern with Christian primary groups. The primary
> groups that arose from ordinary social intercourse provided suffi-
> cient Christian interchange and support. That is no longer true.[2]

Taking this small group dimension as his viewpoint and
model, the priest tends to present Christ to his people as one
who issues a personal invitation to love and freedom rather than
a command to obey a set of laws. He uses, to illustrate this, the
biblical themes which emphasize these values; he sees Christ in
the traditional Jewish roles of social leadership: prophet, priest
and king. In Old Testament days these roles commanded an
obedience to the Lord flowing from one's born membership in
the chosen people called to serve God. The priest sees this same
social reality summed up in Christ's call to the whole of mankind; his invitation to men is a call to love and serve within the
framework of the interracial community of man. The stress is on
individual decision, on freely given faith, and on loving service.

In response to this evolving emphasis, the priest sees himself
and his role differently. In a way that is yet rather vague and
confused, he tries to be a community leader whose task it is to
promote this free and mature acceptance of personal faith in
Christ. He learns from recent literature and, hopefully, from

[2] Charles Davis, *God's Grace in History* (New York: Sheed and Ward,
1966), pp. 67–68.

some study of social psychology and group dynamics that he can best fulfil this task in a community context of openness, mutual listening and shared responsibility. He may remember, from his study of Greek, that the *koinonia* theme of the New Testament meant that the early Christians shared in a kind of community ownership of the Spirit, the message and the gifts of Christ in a communal style of life marked by the mutuality of love and truth. In this social framework of caring and sharing, the only authority is that of Christ calling each person to enter into love and to live in truth; any use of power over others seems foreign, as does any element of personal status or prestige in community leadership. The priest who thinks along these lines feels that he must base his leadership on a full respect for human equality and dignity as he becomes more open to the human reality of those in his Christian group; the use of personal power, moral force, threats of punishment, prestige approaches and "talking down" to people, seem foreign to his whole effort.

THE PRIEST LIVES WITHIN A STRUCTURE OF AUTHORITY

While this liberalizing tendency is gaining force, the priest still remains the official local agent of church authority. It seems inevitable to him that such a large and complex world community as the Roman Catholic church must have a firm set of rules, a clear working order, a chain of command, the power to make the chain workable, and penalities for deviant behavior. I have found, in seminars on this topic, that some priest will always point out, "But there must be someone who ends a discussion, someone to make a final decision, otherwise we get nowhere."

W. J. Sprott points out how very basic to group life is the development of standards and rules:

> The presence of standards of conduct is an essential feature of group interaction because interaction itself cannot go on for long without mutually accepted standards emerging. Standards have two aspects; they are frameworks of expectation and measures of esteem.

If two people interact with one another, each has to adapt his response to the other's, and so to behave that he can foresee what the other will do in response to his response. Theoretically speaking, each of the interacting parties has an enormous repertoire of behavior, any one item of which he can call on at will, but it is obvious that if the behavior of each were entirely random, they could never be said to *inter*-act.[3]

Sprott goes on to point out that two people who belong to the same wider community are already equipped with numerous cultural expectations and rules, but that if they go on to form a friendship, further interpersonal rules and standards will emerge; larger groups develop more complex expectations:

What happens is that, without the participants noticing it, a set of customs becomes established which are regarded as "right" within the context in which the group operates, and they are felt by each member as being in some sense outside himself . . . the group, if it has been in being for a time, assumes a kind of independent existence in the minds of its members, and the rules are ascribed to it.[4]

Often, when a new group is formed for some reason, the members will spend a good deal of time working out a formal set of purposes and rules, which are amended from time to time; less formal groups tend to evolve standards and expectations in the way Sprott describes.

We shall summarise, a little later, what seems to have happened in the evolution of authority in the Church; here it is enough to emphasize that the Church has at present a highly developed authority and rule system, of which the priest is normally the local agent. This authority is conceived vertically, as coming from God rather than from the community itself; it is centered in a self-perpetuating hierarchy of officials who claim a direct historical link through the apostles to the authority of Christ. Whether it is viewed as a monarchical system centered in the Pope, or also as partly oligarchical in the shared authority of

---

[3] W. J. Sprott, *Human Groups* (Harmondsworth, England: Penguin Books, 1958) , pp. 12–13.
[4] *Loc. cit.*

the body of bishops throughout the world, this system of which the priest is a functioning part is highly authoritative. It gives final authority to one person, elected by a small group of men personally appointed by his predecessor. It has a highly developed and well-codified system of law, complete with provision of courts, appeals, penalties, expulsions; appointments within the system are by vertical authority, with only small use of elective procedure. A top level revision of the system has been for some time in process, largely as a result of new principles adopted during the Vatican Council. It seems that this revision will sweep away a great mass of outdated detail without making any very major changes in the vertical lines of authority. In the type of seminar discussion I have referred to, the appeal for clear authority and decision-making is almost inevitably in terms of this vertically conceived system of centralized authority and law; most Catholics, and particularly priests, seem so conditioned to the system that they are incapable of imagining any other way of organizing a community of Christians. This set of mind is generally rationalized in terms of the divinely instituted structure of the Church and its divinely guided history. When it is pointed out that modern scriptural and historical scholarship allows for a great deal of diversity and flexibility in church authority, this is often felt to be irreverent and disloyal.

THE PRIEST LIVES IN ROLE CONFLICT

This emotional involvement in the present authority system highlights the conflict situation of the priest as he tries to be both a promoter of responsible human freedom and the agent of an ancient authority system. The quotation from the Vatican Council with which this chapter begins, provides a strong statement of human freedom: "The exercise of religion consists before all else in those internal, voluntary and free acts whereby man sets the course of his life directly toward God." A dozen pages further on in the same document, we find this firm statement on authority:

> In the formation of their consciences, the Christian faithful ought carefully to attend to the sacred and certain doctrine of the Church. The Church is, by the will of Christ, the teacher of the truth. It is her duty to give utterance to, and authoritatively to teach, that truth which is Christ himself, and also to declare and confirm by her authority those principles of the moral order which have their origin in human nature itself.[5]

The document makes small attempt at any intellectual synthesis of these rather different pictures of the life of a Christian; it seems to make no real effort to consider the emotional conflict of the man-on-the-spot, who may have a deep religious and human involvement in two roles experienced as incompatible.

In the first of these roles, as we have seen, the priest sees himself as a community leader, who, from the position of basic equality indicated by his human involvement, promotes in his various groups of Christians the sense of mature and free responsiveness by which they may listen to Christ's invitation to faith and to mutual love and care. He is widely advised, in carrying out this role, to become a listening person and to be rather non-directive in his group leadership, so as to allow full scope for the dynamics of mutual growth, insight and caring within the group. Even in the larger group of his parish, he is expected to bring these basic attitudes into play, to present the Christian message as a challenge to personal and group decision, to build group life in terms of the mutual care of a shared responsibility and a full respect for the varied competence and functions of the members.

The second role is that of agent of an authoritative Church. While in the above paragraph, the Church seems to be the whole community, in this paragraph it seems to be the Pope and the bishops authoritatively proclaiming a divinely given truth,

[5] Abbott, *op. cit.*, pp. 694–695.

declaring and confirming with full authority from God a set of principles of the moral order. The priest's task is to pass this authoritative message and final declaration of truth and morality on to his people. Here he speaks as a man of authority, as a link in the chain of command, as one whose call is for obedience and a childlike faith.

The only solution offered by the bishops at the Vatican Council is that he should do both. Acting in his first role, he is asked to be a brother to his people, "a brother among brothers." In his second role, he is still to be a father and teacher, and lay people are urged to obey him, and to follow him as their shepherd and father. However relaxed may be his use of authority, he is expected to uphold the authority of bishops and to expound their message. Presumably the priest will find some personal and existential synthesis of these roles through their dynamic interaction in his relationships with his people; he may tend to be somewhat directive in his community leadership and brotherly function, and to be somewhat relaxed and thoughtful in his exercise of authority.

This conflict of roles is, of course, not confined to priests. White and Lippitt, in their study of the psychology of group leadership, discuss the way in which this problem affects parents, teachers, community leaders, personnel directors and politicians:

> One real and ever-present issue is "How much freedom is practical?" Nearly everyone wants freedom up to the point, where, in his eyes, it conflicts "too much" with other values such as law and order, hard work, or group efficiency. But when does it actually conflict, seriously, with these other values? And how much is "too much?" In thousands of concrete situations these are the real issues. Often, of course, the appeal to law and order or to efficiency, as a reason for restricting freedom, is a cover-up; but often, too, it is valid. Abraham Lincoln, to preserve the Union, approved conscription into the Union Army. At one extreme the need for coercive measures which may be called "autocratic" is clear and urgent; at the other extreme, only authoritarian personalities or persons committed to autocratic ideologies fail to see that democratic methods

are preferable. But between the extremes there is a broad zone of genuine uncertainty and legitimate disagreement.[6]

This problem faced by all social leaders in our evolving societies takes on a special sharpness in the life of the Roman Catholic priest. As we discussed in the beginning of this book, the Church is his life, determining his personal identity and, very largely, his social status and roles. He is deeply involved, both intellectually and emotionally, in the tensions of freedom and authority. He experiences the Church's total commitment to human freedom and growth in personal decision more deeply and personally than would be average for the members of other social groups or societies. His experience of the authoritarian character of his Church, too, is likely to be more deep and disturbing than that of members of other groups who come to see the need for group authority.

REJECTION OF THE DOUBLE ROLE

The adding together of the priest's two roles and their mutual interaction, as outlined in the Vatican Council and in much modern writing on the priest, seems to be rejected by an increasing number of priests and lay people. In many cases this rejection takes the form of such a strong emphasis on one or other role that the other, while theoretically allowed for, is practically excluded. The existential synthesis chosen by many priests is very often of this type; the choice made seems to operate in terms of a selective perception of personal and group realities, which may stem from basic patterns of personality development. This practical rejection of an admitted role at the personal level is parallelled by many recent public statements from church authorities which seem only to add to the role confusion of the priest, and by much current writing on the work of the priest-

[6] Ralph K. White and Ronald Lippitt, *Autocracy and Democracy* (New York: Harper and Brothers, 1960), p. 4.

hood. By contrast, the needed work of attempting a new synthesis seems to be attracting little attention.

More study and research is required on the psychological problems of the double role, particularly on the anxieties and inner disharmony created by the kind of practical role rejection we have looked at. The priest who has really opted for one role as dominant is often only pretending to carry out the other. This may mean that he has brought deep elements of unreality and fantasy into the central experience of life and its meaning, and into the very structure of his personal identity. This seems, in many cases in which I have been involved as counselor, to engender uneasy feelings of anxiety, inadequacy, and generalized guilt and unworthiness.

White and Lippitt discuss in detail the differing social needs that may be satisfied in democratic and autocratic groups, and the personality stresses that may be involved. They emphasize above all the importance of clarity of role and role expectation:

> *Clearness* of roles and role-expectations is as important for satisfaction as it is for group efficiency. Confusion and needlessly prolonged indecision, as in the laissez-faire experimental situations, are important aspects of the kind of "freedom" from which most people want to escape. They are bad enough in themselves; they are worse when misunderstanding of what others expect results in compounding confusion with ill will. Where clearness of roles calls for frank recognition of an inherently autocratic power structure, or of the inherently autocratic elements in an otherwise democratic power structure, it is still far superior to a blurring of perception of that structure by a pretense of being "democratic." [7]

All will surely agree that honesty and clarity of role is essential for good group functioning; the difficulty in the case of the priest is that both roles seem to be authentic and essential to him, and that the blurring and confusion seem inevitable.

This is the familiar double bind situation of which we spoke earlier. Here is a man caught in a conflict decision in which he

[7] *Ibid.,* p. 259.

seems to be in trouble whichever way he moves. In this typical situation, a man is bound by a strong emotional bond or dependency in such a way that he cannot escape his anxiety or guilt. The situation is similar to the case of an adolescent wanting to go out with his friends, and being told by his loving, possessive, "martyr-complexed" mother: "Certainly you go and have a good time with the boys; I'll be quite all right on my own here all day." The boy vaguely realizes that she is telling him one thing and meaning the opposite, that he is going to be blamed and to feel guilty whichever decision he makes. If he did not love his mother so much it would not be so difficult. Often his dilemma is only heightened by the further ambiguity of a denial that there is any problem, as when his mother adds: "But there's no problem, really, darling. You shouldn't worry about me so much. You're a big boy now, and you have to lead your own life." With his total life involvement in the work of the Church, the priest realizes that it is essential for him to be promoting freedom and mature responsibility in his people, and equally essential that he be faithful to the authority statements of bishops, which so often seem to conflict with his first aim. When he is assured that there is no problem if he is only a loyal son of the Church, we have the typical double bind which we have described.

LEADER OF A CONFUSED LAITY

These psychological difficulties of the priest in carrying out a double role are, of course, matched by those of the lay people in responding to his role. The role of lay people in the Church is, to a large extent, complementary to that of the priest; the mutual interaction of these roles is often forgotten. When, for example, the bishops at the Vatican Council decided on an upgrading of the position, dignity and responsibility of lay people in the functioning of the Church, they seemed to give little attention to the consequent modifications in the role of the clergy. The ambiguity we have stressed in the role of priests is mirrored in the experience of perceptive lay people in adapting to their new role of responsibility in the Church. They have sensed that while bishops and priests are emphasizing the mature freedom of lay people which the Vatican Council described and the need for them to assume a wide responsibility in church affairs and discussions, the old hierarchical attitudes continue to persist. Bishops and priests are demanding from the laity a response of childlike submissiveness and obedience to church authority even in these new modalities of responsible freedom.

Terence Eagleton, in a chapter in *The New Left Church* entitled "Priesthood and Paternalism," makes an analysis of this situation, which he describes as liberal paternalism. He discusses a general failure in the social thinking of Christians which he traces to a fundamental commitment to the status quo; this leads to a tendency to avoid any radical thinking, to present social comment at a simple level or only in wide and safe generalizations, as in papal encyclicals. He describes British society as working its way through an evolution from the idea of authoritarianism as the dominant model of human relationship to that of democracy, and relates the present intervening stage of liberal paternalism to the present situation of laity and clergy within the Church. He describes the typical patterns of this stage of development as an attempt on the part of the old authorities to meet radical claims by a good deal of concession in such a way that the basic authority structure is not changed, but may be even reinforced.

Eagleton outlines the view the layman receives of the double role of the priest and bishop as they promote freedom and emphasize authority:

> The church is undergoing its own version of the liberal-paternalist crisis. When any movement for renewal starts up, there are always anxious hands available ready to catch it up and make it

harmless under the plea of guidance and control; the plea may be genuine, but the damage can be severe. The hands are there, hovering, each time we are told to play down our differences in the interests of a public image; each time our common heritage as catholics is made into a blunt instrument to compel submission and compromise masquerading as prudence and loyalty. Protest and dissent is accepted, but changed in tone and emphasis so that it can blend into an only slightly modified status quo. . . . The problem, with church and society, is how to meet and satisfy demands from "below" without relinquishing real power, without opening the floodgates to basic structural change. The language used, in progressive catholic circles, is significant of this: "consultation" with the laity, lay "participation" in the church. "Consultation" is the familiar paternalist word: it suggests the General de Gaulle technique of bending a kindly ear without any ultimate necessity to accept the opinions of those consulted; it suggests, more deeply, that the policy-making remains in traditional hands, but the policy-makers are now more willing to listen to constructive proposals from outside. This is also what "participation" can suggest: sharing in processes which remain ultimately the monopoly of others. The liberal paternalism is mystifying and self-justifying . . . there is something a little odd in being consulted about things which are one's own business in the first place.[8]

An example of the liberal-paternal technique that is almost amusing is that used in recent years by the Roman Curia, the headquarters staff of the Church in Rome. During the Vatican Council, there was a strong feeling expressed by the bishops in criticism of the curia for its authoritarian ways; numerous resolutions and measures passed by the bishops were interpreted as a call for the decentralizing of church authority from the curia to the boards of bishops in each country. It seemed that the position of the curia, as the entrenched and self-perpetuating center of church authority, had been dramatically weakened. Yet now, three years after the close of the council, the curia seems stronger than ever; it has made itself the indispensable agent of promoting, verifying and authenticating the bishops' efforts at church renewal, so that the general effect has been an

[8] Terence Eagleton, *The New Left Church* (Baltimore: Helicon, 1966), pp. 100–102.

upgrading and expansion of the work and personnel of the curia. From local knowledge of many areas in the English-speaking world, one could guess that a similar decentralizing and strengthening process has also been going on in local church affairs. The net result, for priests as well as lay people, is, as Eagleton puts it, mystifying and self-justifying. Certainly, the general effect of adding the new aspects of the role of the priest to the older traditional aspects seems to result in a general confusion of roles and role expectations.

Similar confusion and mutual suspicion has been widely reported in areas of industry where elements of joint consultation, profit-sharing and worker participation in planning have been introduced without any basic redistribution of power and authority. Trade unionists have been generally wary of such measures which may have a net effect of strengthening the overall position of management and of confusing the traditional aims of the workers. Here again, there is a kind of instinctive rejection of the simple combining of somewhat incompatible roles without a new synthesis of the basic structure of power and authority. It may well be, in many such cases, that neither party is as yet ready for the major changes which such a new synthesis might involve.

DENIAL OF THE PROBLEM

Such a general unreadiness may well be a strong factor in the kind of tacit collusion by which members of the Roman Catholic church tend to avoid discussion of the basic roles within the Church and the responsibilities which might correspond to them. Many commentators have commented on this kind of collusion, by which a social group sets itself up, in reality, as a generalized defense system against the possibility of basic change. It seems that members in all ranks, by a kind of unconscious understanding, fortify themselves and the group against the anxieties and redefinitions of identity and function that a basic change might occasion. In place of discussion of these challenges, a great deal of busywork is generated in terms of relatively harmless changes, which are then hailed as major steps forward. It seems that this kind of group process was operating strongly at the Vatican Council, which conspicuously avoided a number of major issues in favor of a great deal of relatively harmless renewal. We have seen that any really searching discussion of the roles of the priest was among the many areas avoided; this avoidance continues within the Church, as if by some general agreement it has been decided that if we keep everyone busy about small problems, the big ones will go away.

This chapter may seem rather negative in stressing from many viewpoints the rather inevitable character of a seemingly hopeless role conflict. This stress is necessary because of the importance of seeing that there is a problem. To a sociologist or social psychologist reading this chapter, the matter may seem obvious enough and familiar enough. By reason of the very mechanisms of problem denial which we have looked at in the last few pages, the matter will not seem obvious to most Catholics or to most priests, and may be felt by some of them as rather shocking. I myself have been described as "courageous and outspoken" so many times that I could almost come to believe it. I have to remind myself that if I were to write a similar analysis on the role conflicts of social workers or family counselors, my book might be praised for its perceptiveness, but scarcely for its courage. What should I be afraid of, and whom would I be fighting?

The paternalist attitudes of those in church authority lead them to assure us that all will be well if we leave the worrying and planning to them; there are no problems, really, which loyalty and goodness and obedience will not easily solve—and we must all be patient, and not try to do too much too quickly. It can become particularly wearisome for priests like myself, and for lay people with similar interests, to have to spend so much time trying to prove within the church group that problems do exist, particularly when our friends who are psychologists or sociologists or intelligent humanists can recognize these problems immediately and go on to discussion and argument with us. Eagleton, in his discussion of church roles, describes his experience:

> To understand the nature of Christian roles and relationships, then, we must get some idea of what this liberal-paternalist crisis really is, and this is difficult in the first place because part of the crisis is the assurance, at times, that there isn't really one at all. It is, in other words, a crisis of consciousness which refuses to become fully self-conscious because to do so might be a kind of self-destruction. A large part of our attention and energy must therefore be directed simply to naming and identifying the crisis, discerning the actual truth of our social condition.[9]

We have seen, then, some of the elements of role conflict which affect the priest in this area of authority, and some of the psychological and sociological problems which militate against the current style of dealing with the conflict. We can go on, in the next chapter, to review the positive forces working in the Church at present towards a new synthesis of freedom and authority. We shall see that this reformulating of the authority role of the priest is as yet tentative and incomplete, but that substantial progress has been made in terms of the necessary scriptural and historical studies, and some interesting beginnings made in terms of practical role situations within the present church structures.

[9] *Ibid.*, p. 90.

6: CARRYING THE
WEIGHT OF HISTORY
/ some new ways in authority

The role of the priest is rooted not only in the ongoing social reality of the present day but also in the historical reality of the person of Christ and of the development of the Christian Church. Every role in our society is in process of change, and every role has its own history contributing to its evolution. In some cases the history is short and not very formative, for example that of experts in industrial management, and it is comparatively easy for these roles to evolve flexibly to meet the changing reality they serve. The role of the social worker, on the other hand, is evolving only with difficulty, burdened as it is with a history of nineteenth century benevolence and charity work rather imperfectly assimilated into the modern style of community planning, group dynamics and personal service.

In the case of the Roman Catholic priest, the identification of his role with history is particularly strong and expressive. His identity and function within the Church and in the wider community takes shape in relation to the person and deeds of Christ and the history of his followers through the centuries. For this reason, the reshaping of the present-day role of the priest must take into account the whole social history of priesthood in the communities of the West. We must look at the social history of the authority role of the priest to see some of its inner meaning and the root forces of its ongoing tensions. This inner view should help us to evaluate better some of the more recent developments reported in this area of the priest's life.

HISTORY OF THE PRIEST'S AUTHORITY ROLE

The general role of the Catholic priest and the source of his authority function can be traced back to the social roles of prophet, priest and king in the Old Testament period of Jewish life. It is evident from the New Testament writings that the early followers of Christ conceived his mission in terms of these three traditional roles. As the leadership roles of the early Christian communities were clarified, they were seen in terms of an identity with Christ and his mission to the world. Through all the social conditioning of the priest role during the history of Christianity, this identification remains a stable factor. This is the frame of reference within which we are able to outline the way in which the authority role of the priest has been conditioned by the influence of history.

There is an increasing emphasis in recent studies of the Catholic church on this factor of historical development and conditioning; the theological discussion of process theories of reality has a relevance to the priest's role which we will emphasize later. Karl Rahner, a theologian who takes a middle view in this discussion, distinguishes the ongoing concrete reality of the Church from its unchanging, essential constitution:

> the church's awareness of her constitution has a history, just as much as her dogma and her understanding of faith. As this awareness lives by her continuing, spontaneous life, so it has in its development and history also an influence on the concrete life of the church. Furthermore, the constantly changing external historical situation of the church demands a constant renewal of the concrete expressions of her permanent, essential structure, corresponding to

the conditions of the particular time, because in fact also the real essence of the church (which is something more than the idea of her essence) always exists in man as contingent and historical and in the church's historically conditioned action.[1]

Taking for the present, then, this moderate view of the dynamism of history in the shaping of the Church and its institutions, we look first at the authority role of Christ as seen by his followers in the first century of the life of the Christian Church. We may use this view of Christ as a frame of reference as we see the historical evolution of the authority of the priest through the centuries and lead up to the present situation and its trends. The authenticity of these trends must certainly be judged in relation to the general social movements and developments of our time, but, since the role in question is that of the Christian priest, they must be judged also in relation to the role of Christ as described in the New Testament.

THE AUTHORITY POSITION OF CHRIST

When we examine the New Testament writings from this viewpoint, we see Christ clearly as an anti-authority figure. There is a long-continuing discussion as to whether he can properly be called a revolutionary figure. Since his practical program of action for himself and his followers did not include any immediate reform of social structures, his mission is better described in terms of a revolutionary ideal rather than a revolutionary program. He showed a highly critical and anti-authoritarian attitude to the social and religious leaders of his society, and the picture of his public life which we have in the gospels shows him on an inevitable collision course with them.

The startling character of all this has been smoothed over by the piety of the centuries. It is easy now to forget that Christ

[1] Karl Rahner, *Bishops: Their Status and Function* (Baltimore: Helicon, 1964), pp. 14–15.

was regarded by responsible authorities of his time as a danger to social order and authority and as a fanatic who was against religion. Although there is much ambiguity about some of his recorded sayings, there is no doubt as to the general theme of his attack on authority. St. Luke's gospel begins with a vision of a new order. We read a prophetic proclamation coming from his mother, Mary, in which traditional themes of Jewish religious and social reform are woven together in the name of God, depicted as exercising his power and fulfilling the promises made to Abraham:

> he has done valiantly with the strength of his arm, driving the proud astray in the conceit of their hearts; he has put down the mighty from their seat, and exalted the lowly; he has filled the hungry with good things, and sent the rich away empty-handed (Luke 1:51-53).

Many incidents in the life of Christ show him as rejecting a political role for himself and his followers; the constant stress is on the formation of a brotherhood of believers who will be a new kind of human community, the model for a future age. The critical message against authority, as we look more deeply, is an emphasis on the mutuality of persons, on the dignity of the individual, and on the notion of leadership as a loving service which confers no higher status, but rather a lower one. This is set in contrast with the social structure and functioning of the religious and civil authority of the time.

In the ever continuing dichotomy of social reform and renewal, Christ comes nearer the anarchist model than that of the power revolutionary. Woodcock, in his study of anarchism, describes its ideal this way:

> The great anarchists call on us to stand on our own moral feet like a generation of princes, to become aware of justice as an inner fire, and to learn that the still, small voices of our own hearts speak

more truly than the choruses of propaganda that daily assault our outer ears. "Look into the depths of your own beings," said Peter Arshinov, the friend of Makhno. "Seek out the truth and realize it yourselves. You will find it nowhere else." In this insistence that freedom and moral self-realization are interdependent, and one cannot live without the other, lies the ultimate lesson of true anarchism.[2]

Although there are many ways in which Christ's teaching differs from that of the classical anarchists, one thing that is similar is the vision of a model community, loving and serving one another as brothers and equals. The attitude of Christ to authority is seen in the leadership training which he gave to his immediate followers and in the way in which he handled problems of group conflict and dominance.

The gospel of Matthew describes the mother of James and John requesting a high place in the kingdom for her sons, and the hostility shown by the other ten apostles. Jesus told them:

> You know that, among the Gentiles, those who bear rule lord it over them, and great men vaunt their power over them; with you it must be otherwise; whoever would be a great man among you, must be your servant, and whoever has a mind to be first among you must be your slave. So it is that the son of man did not come to have service done him, he came to serve others (Matthew 20: 25–28).

Luke has this conflict and lesson in the setting of the final Passover meal, with Christ saying:

> The kings of the Gentiles lord it over them, and those who bear rule over them win the name of benefactors. With you it is not to be so; no difference is to be made, among you, between the greatest and the youngest of all, between him who commands and him who serves. Tell me, which is greater, the man who sits at table, or the man who serves him? Surely the man who sits at table: yet I am here among you as your servant (Luke 22:24–27).

McKenzie, in his recent study of church authority from the viewpoint of scriptural scholarship, sums the matter up in this way:

[2] George Woodcock, *Anarchism* (Cleveland: Meridian, 1962), pp. 450–451.

The New Testament is anti-authoritarian in a proper sense. It abhors that type of domination which in the New Testament world was seen in secular power or in religious autocracy. It is anti-authoritarian in the sense that it permits no member of the church to occupy a position of dignity and eminence; the first in the church must be the lackey and the slave of others, and may strive for no dignity and eminence except in dedication to service in love. The New Testament uses words to describe church officers which place them on the lowest social level known in the Roman-Hellenistic world of the first century.[3]

McKenzie comments at length (pp. 24–33) on power and authority in the life of Christ, relating the power to his working of miracles and the authority to the authenticity of his message from God; he deals exhaustively with the shades of meaning conveyed in the use of the word "diakonia," translated usually as service, and concludes by pointing out that Jesus gave no clear instructions for a constitution of his church brotherhood. He was only emphatic that it should not be governed on the model of the secular power of that time. His commission to his followers was rather for them to find forms and structures appropriate for a new kind of human association, a group based on love and care.

From the sociological viewpoint, then, we see Christ as a charismatic leader figure with an anti-authoritarian message. He keeps himself free from the power situation of his time and refuses to make any political or military bid for power. He gathers followers around him by the power of his miracles, by his sure sense of the authenticity of his message, by the magic of his personality, and by his deep, loving concern for those in need. He gives to his followers no clear-cut plan, but rather a vision of a sharing and caring fellowship of mutual love and concern, marked by the equality of brotherhood. In all this, Christ is following the general pattern of charismatic leadership: the man with a mission who rises outside the authority structures of society and defines his purposes basically in personal rather than

[3] John L. McKenzie, *Authority in the Church* (New York: Sheed and Ward, 1966) , p. 84.

structural terms. We have seen the way in which Christ was identified with the prophets of the Jewish past. The terms in which he appropriated also the functions of kingship and priesthood into the loose framework of his brotherhood of love provide one of the startling innovations in the establishment of Christianity. Here we have the three traditional roles, each claiming a divine mission, re-centered in one person and given over to a new interpersonal idealism of love and concern.

Max Weber, in a chapter on the sociology of the world religions, makes a study of the charismatic leader, and describes his power as

> a rule over men, whether predominantly external or predominantly internal, to which the governed submit because of their belief in the extraordinary quality of the specific *person* . . . the legitimacy of their rule rests on the belief in and the devotion to the extraordinary, which is valued because it goes beyond the normal human qualities, and which was originally valued as supernatural . . . charismatic rule is not managed according to general norms, either traditional or rational, but, in principle, according to concrete revelations and inspirations, and in this sense, charismatic authority is "irrational." It is "revolutionary" in the sense of not being bound to the existing order: "It is written—but I say unto you . . . !" [4]

AUTHORITY IN THE APOSTOLIC COMMUNITIES

It is only slowly that we find, in the later New Testament writings, patterns of group leadership beginning to emerge. This leadership centers around the apostles as official witnesses to the sayings and deeds of Christ, although Paul, a later convert and not a direct witness, seems easily to gain a kind of equality with the others. Emphasis seems to be on face-to-face relationships in primary groups. We see group-sharing of decisions, responsibilities and, to some extent, community goods and services. The

[4] *From Max Weber: Essays in Sociology,* edited H. H. Gerth and C. Wright Mills (New York: Oxford University Press, 1946) , pp. 295–296.

constant stress seems to be on persons rather than structures, on love, service and responsibility rather than on authority and obedience. There is a pervasive emphasis on freedom and on liberation from law. Throughout these early community writings, there is a notably brief time perspective and a joyful expectation of the coming again of Christ in majesty to end this present world of time. Perhaps it is only as this expectation fades that the problems of more permanent structures for the church communities became evident.

The wide variety of functions and the lack of formal structure is shown in the description of the church in Corinth provided in Paul's first epistle to this local group (see especially chapters 11–14). Here Paul is evaluating the various charisms and functions, centering his praise and attention on love as the greatest gift, the one without which all others are valueless. McKenzie makes a study of the various offices and functions of the Pauline churches, and concludes:

> The impression which the early church leaves of itself is that it was very tolerant of variation in form and function; there is no clear deliberate effort to reach fixity of structure. The office and the function can be modified to meet existing situations; there are many gifts, but one Spirit. The structure itself is not sacred; the inner life which gives the structure its Christian character is sacred.[5]

It is in the post-apostolic period that we see emerging into clear definition the present traditional roles of the officers of the Christian Church: the bishop, the priest and the deacon. It is important for our consideration of the role of the priest to recognize that while the priest role was implicit in the Church from the beginning and is clearly part of the identification of Christ's role and mission, it emerged into clear definition precisely at the time when the Christian communities were assuming their permanent structures.

---

[5] McKenzie, *op. cit.*, pp. 76–77.

THE AUTHORITY ROLE IN THE DEVELOPMENT OF STRUCTURE

Max Weber describes this process of the formalizing of the charismatic elements of a group in terms of the formation of social strata and the need of those in the upper strata to have their position legitimized in acquired and sanctified rights. We see a process in which the original charismatic elements become objectified within a structure of domination. Weber continues:

> Genuine charisma is absolutely opposed to this objectified form. It does not appeal to an enacted or traditional order, nor does it base its claims upon acquired rights. Genuine charisma rests upon the legitimation of personal heroism or personal revelation. Yet precisely this quality of charisma as an extraordinary, supernatural, divine power transforms it, after its routinization, into a suitable source for the legitimate acquisition of sovereign power by the successors of the charismatic hero.[6]

We experience a sense of fatal inevitability as we follow the history of church structure through the early centuries, and see, with the building of the necessary social forms for the ordering of a larger society, the loss of so many of the elements of spontaneity, social equality and shared responsibility, which seemed essential to the early Christian message on authority. A hope had been offered of a new kind of human grouping based on equality, brotherhood and mutual care; what we see developing is an ecclesiastical caste system in which the bishops and priests, and, later on, the monks become socially more and more separated from lay people. We see the officials of the Church becoming a distinct social group, borrowing from the dominant Roman and Greek cultures of the Mediterranean the formal styles of authority, law, upper-class learning and personal domination. All of this is still cloaked in the language of the New Testament, and, no doubt, much of the underlying reality of the church fellowship remains intact. However, the privileges of the by now full-

6 Gerth and Mills, *op. cit.,* p. 262.

time functionaries and the legitimation of their separate position becomes one of the chief concerns of the new ecclesiastical
learning which marks them apart.

Many church historians, while noting this tendency, feel
that it is inevitable that the Church would adopt the social
styles of the culture in which it took root, so that we see in turn
an imperial age in the Church, a monarchical period, a feudal
period, a bureaucratic period, and so on. It is precisely this inevitability which is being widely questioned in the discussion of
the authority role of the priest in our own day. One of the important effects of the modern return to the sources of Christian
life in the Bible is the increasing criticism of the present-day social forms of church authority. These forms are now open to
judgment by the standards of the New Testament. Many modern priests and lay people are suggesting that, whatever the case
in the past, we should no longer accept the inevitability of the
Church using the social authority models of the day for its own
life; we might rather try to live by the ideals of the New Testament, at whatever cost, and present a new working model of
group life to the world of men. While the reality of church life
at present is much more confused between the two ends of the
argument than this analysis suggests, the modern priest, in
searching for an authentic role for himself, is deeply concerned
in this discussion of historical conditioning.

The evolution from the leadership of an active and responsible brotherhood to authoritarian rule during the pre-medieval
period is outlined fully in Müller's treatment of church authority. He discusses the various key figures in this development, and
the progressive identification of the rule of the bishop with the
rule of God. He concludes that

> towards the end of the third century—that is even before the great
> change in the political situation of the church—the apostolic minis-
> try has fully evolved towards the monarchical-collegial episcopate.
> The position of the bishop is sharply distinguished from that of the
> layman, and the conception of the church is increasingly confined

to the hierarchy, while the community's active participation in ecclesial concerns as well as its charismatic offices survive only in the Eastern mystical tradition of the "spiritual man." [7]

Müller goes on to describe the general effect of the growth of monasticism in the West and of the assimilation of the life of priests to that of the monks, culminating in the general law of celibacy for all priests. He considers that this fusion of the two areas of church life into one "ecclesiastical state" led to further separation from the laity and their general exclusion from the active life of the Church.

THE AUTHORITARIAN LEGACY OF THE MIDDLE AGES

It was an unscholarly Catholic custom in the days of my youth to idealize the Middle Ages as a golden time of Catholic faith and practice, and to speak of the "thirteenth, the greatest of centuries." Only a little reading in history was necessary to demythologize this view. With a more objective understanding of the tensions of medieval life came the realization of how much of present-day church structure and mythology had its genesis in the social and political energies of medieval Europe.

The highly structured style of social authority and formalized obedience in feudal Europe, which seems so stable on paper, was the center of a perennial power conflict. We find the church leaders—popes and bishops—entering fully into this power game, seeking for themselves secure positions from which to exercise their moral leadership and to pursue their vision of a Christian order of society. Personal qualities of ambition, and the tendency to dominate others, were understandable and, indeed, a great advantage to the church leader in this exercise of power politics. We can be often surprised at the hardy survival of the original Christian message through this period; we are

[7] Alois Müller, *Obedience in the Church* (Westminster, Md.: Newman, 1966) , p. 39.

not surprised that this survival often centers around such charismatic leaders as Francis of Assisi and Catherine of Siena.

In the course of this struggle for power we see popes, bishops and abbots become feudal princes in their own territory, or, as in England, take a seat in the House of Lords. Mcantime the priests, the minor clergy, sought their security by aiming at a set place in the gentry class with all its privileges and its emerging independence of the system. This whole struggle for position became in many places and times a struggle of Church against laity, and the social separation of the priest from the people received new emphasis. This separation was structured into separate legal systems, forms of address and clothing, and a whole separated life style for the clergy. The exercise of the authority role of the priest gradually took on an authoritarian form and a legalistic style which demanded social distance for its exercise and survival. This authority style was further formalized in worship, now almost monopolized by the officiating priest, and in church teaching, expressed increasingly in a command-obedience relationship.

The later centuries of European history, through the Renaissance, the Reformation and the Enlightenment, did little to change the basic positions of priest and laity, and contributed much to their hardening. The divine right theory of social leadership, in which there was much mutual borrowing between religious myth and political absolutism, contributed greatly to the self-image of bishops and priests in legitimizing their separate, nonresponsible position of authority. The breakup of the identity between ecclesiastical and social structures tended to put the priest into a defensive role, in which he became the shepherd guarding his sheep from all the evils of the time, erecting separate safety structures within which they could "practice their faith" as long as they were loyal to their leaders.

The more recent development of bureaucracy in politics and of large-scale management in economics had its parallel in the inner life of the Roman Catholic church. The role development we have just outlined provided a ready-made vehicle for bureaucratic government of church affairs. In this final aspect of the historical conditioning of church life we reach the point of full contrast which sets the stage for the present-day conflict in the authority role of the priest. On one side of the contrast is the revived New Testament model of the Church as a brotherhood based on equality, diversified function, and mutual love and care; on the other side, the present-day Church with its authoritarian power style, its bureaucratic functioning, its complex legal system and its paternalist and impersonal group attitudes. The priest, as local community leader and the agent of the centralized authority system, finds himself doubting his authenticity as he meditates on the New Testament model. And because this kind of thinking is not encouraged within any bureaucracy, the priest doubts whether he should doubt; the more that critical questioning appears in the open, the more the higher church officials appeal to the loyalty of their servants. Once again, we see the priest in a familiar double bind situation.

McKenzie's *Authority in the Church* covers precisely the kind of thoughtful judgment of modern church life by the authority ideal of the New Testament which we have suggested is going on beneath the surface. It verbalizes the conflict situation of the priest and has a powerful appeal by the quality of its scriptural scholarship and the moderation of its tone. McKenzie stresses that he does not consider the New Testament ideal of authority as terminal but as a measure of authenticity; there must be development in authority as in other areas of church life. He writes:

> Such development is a human process and is subject to human fault and failure. As we shall see, very few of the forms which authority takes in the modern church have antecedents in the New Testament; evolution of form has been constant since the apostolic period. Weighed in the balance of history and theology, most of these forms appear to be phenomena which the church produces

and which the church can take away . . . the test of whether any particular form of authority is a genuine development must ultimately be the New Testament, for it is in this document that the original grant of authority to the church is seen.[8]

McKenzie's consideration of charisma and prophecy leads him to see the modern Church in terms of present-day models of organization and establishment, in which routine and mediocrity are canonized and prophecy suppressed. He concludes:

> when an organization has become rigid, it is extremely difficult to tolerate deviations of any kind. We protect a rigid organization because we have never learned to manage a flexible organization. We have identified the organization with the church so closely that anything which seems to point out a defect in the organization or to suggest a modification in structure or administration is taken as an attack on the church itself.[9]

This brief review of the priest's authority role has led us to another point of understanding of the conflict and confusion surrounding the function of the modern clergy. As we have approached the study of this function from various viewpoints, we have come to a rather diffuse analysis of the tensions and dichotomies of one of the more unusual role situations of our modern society. The historical approach of this chapter may serve to give a background of meaning for many current discussions on the details of the life of the clergy. It may appear trivial to argue as to whether a bishop should be called "My Lord" or "Your Excellency," or as to whether a priest should offer worship in the formal clothing of a Roman patrician; the question of the separated life style of the priest, and particularly of his legalized celibacy, may well appear to a neutral observer as much ado about nothing.

Compared with the larger needs of the world of men, and with the outward aims of the Church, these are indeed organizational trivia. But it is precisely one of the central problems of

8 McKenzie, *op. cit.*, pp. 13–14.
9 *Ibid.*, p. 160.

the role of the modern priest that, because of the historical roots of these trivialities, and the large investment in them by way of group emotion and social fixation, so much time and energy must be absorbed in considerations of this kind. It is a common sign of a moribund social group that this kind of internal maintenance energy far outweighs the energy released for the original outward aim of the group. By this sociological standard, the Roman Catholic church must be near to dying of its own weight; this possibility is becoming increasingly evident to the more perceptive of the clergy. This throws a further element of doubt and confusion into the area of the priest's authority role. Not only is he confused as to where he should stand—as a modern style group leader, a medieval authoritarian bureaucrat, or in between as a liberal-paternal figure of ambiguity—but he is often enough not really sure that his main energy should be anywhere in this area. His central confusion may linger around the doubt as to whether the present organizational and authority forms of the Church, in which he is the functioning middleman, have any survival value for the twenty-first century.

7:NEW TASKS FOR THE
PRIEST / *the signs of change*

The disengagement of the Roman Catholic church from the social myth of Christendom has been proceeding unevenly over
the past two or three centuries. The dream of a Christianized
social order in which Church and State might work hand in
hand for the common spiritual and material welfare of the people in a modified theocracy with the Pope as spiritual overlord
was a very fascinating prospect for churchmen in medieval Europe. Much of the higher level thinking within the Church operated on the understanding that this was the will of God and
the authentic meaning of Christianity. For centuries after this
had ceased to be a political possibility it remained the working
image in Rome. The process of disengagement went ahead more
quickly in the Protestant area of Europe and in the new world
of the North American continent, and, later, of the South Pacific. It proceeded more slowly in the Catholic nations of Europe
and in the areas which they colonized. The medieval dream attached to itself in these areas much of the Roman legend of past
empire and universal law; in them the modern Roman absolutism, with the pervasive political influence of cardinals, papal
legates and curial departments, gave to the ancient dream some
air of a surviving, if decaying, reality.

It was not surprising that all of this had little relevance for
the smaller Catholic communities working out their practical

problems of growth and social adjustment within the expanding nations of northern Europe and the worldwide group of English-speaking societies. In the third world of the Asian and African peoples Christianity was originally experienced as a missionary effort which brought many of the benefits of European trade and learning. As these peoples emerge into nationhood, Christianity is being scornfully rejected as part of the colonial past, or it is being built into the evolving national structure according to new models.

The chief work of the recent Vatican Council revolved around this conflict of myth and evolving reality within the Church. On paper, at least, it seems that the myth was finally written out. The lengthy arguments and political plays centering around the council's document on religious liberty were a symptom of the energies and emotions involved in this conflict situation. The delay in approving this document was incomprehensible to many neutral observers, and, indeed, to many priests. It seemed such a harmless statement, emphasizing so mildly human dignities and religious liberties which our countries had adopted so long ago that they were forgotten issues. To many priests of my acquaintance it was deeply disturbing to realize that they were officials of a Church whose bishops were not very sure that they believed in religious liberty.

John Courtney Murray, the American theologian who was one of the chief backroom architects of this document, acknowledges the historical lateness of the Church's enthusiasm for freedom:

> It can hardly be maintained that the declaration is a milestone in human history—moral, political, or intellectual. The principle of religious freedom has long been recognized in constitutional law, to the point where even Marxist-Leninist political ideology is obliged to pay lip-service to it. In all honesty it must be admitted that the church is late in acknowledging the validity of the principle.[1]

[1] *Documents of Vatican II*, Walter M. Abbott, editor (New York: Guild, America and Association Presses, 1966), p. 673.

We have seen in an earlier chapter (pp. 81, 86) some quotations from this document and have noted the confusions and ambiguities it engenders for the practical role of the priest. While the document avoids the controversial area of the exercise of religious freedom within the Catholic church, it bears strong implications in terms of the primacy of human conscience and man's basic freedom before God. These implications were noted by Murray in his commentary quoted above; he points out that the great argument on the meaning of Christian freedom within the Church is now beginning. Because the currents of this argument affect the role of the priest so deeply, we must look at the directions it is taking at present.

The Vatican Council several times reiterates a strong claim for an absolute moral and religious authority over members of the Church, an authority wholly in the hands of the Pope and bishops. At the same time, its acceptance of the principles of religious freedom, and of the ideal of a free man before God in a free society, clearly recognizes a countertendency which implies the final rejection of the old dream of a church-dominated social structure and of the autocratic use of authority within the Church. It stresses the ideals of brotherhood, fellowship and collegiality in the life of the Church. It discusses, rather inconclusively, Christ's attitudes to authority and service, and his warnings against the use of dominant authority and personal power. All of this tendency, while still ambiguous enough not to create any immediate disturbance of the centralized power situation in the Church, represents the intrusion into an authoritarian bureaucracy of dynamic elements of change and evolution. These elements have their source in many of the movements of modern thought which were discussed in the early pages of this book; from these movements they are gaining strength and vitality. While, as we have seen, they are experienced for the present by many priests in terms of role confusion, they represent the positive elements of change and renewal which, hopefully, may lead to a new synthesis on the role and function of the priest.

SOCIOLOGY INFLUENCING THE CHURCH

Sociology and social psychology provide the strongest of the influences for change in the structure and roles of the Church. More and more of the clergy, as well as great numbers of lay people, are coming, in the course of higher education, to study the meaning of community, of status and role, of social function; they are becoming familiar with concepts of democracy and autocracy, of bureaucracy and group responsibility, of group dynamics and various forms of leadership. It is inevitable that much of the modern reflection on the life of the Church is being made from this viewpoint; many of the ideals of the New Testament concerning group life, mutual care and community responsibility are being seen with a new practicality, as new working models emerge within the life of the wider community.

The Church has experienced its group life in the light of many models through the centuries. Some of these derive from the New Testament and have taken on a continuing life through a historical development. The monarchic model has been the most influential of these; the Church is seen as the kingdom of God, and its leaders as governors and princes, making laws in the name of God. The paternal model sees the Church as the adopted family of God, with God as our Father, and church leaders exercising a fatherly authority over their children. The magisterial model presents the Church as a school; God sends his Son to teach all nations, and he passes on this teaching authority to popes and bishops, who instruct, govern and discipline their pupils according to various older theories and styles of pedagogy. Numerous studies in sociology and social psychology point to the way in which these forms of leadership can evolve into autocratic and bureaucratic forms in large groups through various dynamisms of submissiveness in the led, and power-seeking in the leader; often, too, a crisis situation will seem to demand a strong leader with total authority, and this sets a continuing pattern. Our discussion of historical conditioning showed the way in which the Church tends to adopt social patterns of authority; the autocratic tendencies in modern church life have had imperial, monarchic, feudal, bureaucratic and dictatorial models to follow and improve on. In our own day, the managerial revolution offers a new model for a new style autocrat to experiment with.

Of special interest to sociologists is the way that the Church has been reemphasizing countermodels in recent times. The New Testament image of Christ as our elder brother has received a growing attention over the past thirty years or so, preparing the way for a fraternal model for church life to be adopted by the Vatican Council. Its decree on the life of priests lays stress on this image, describing the Church as a brotherhood in which priests are "brothers among brothers." A functional model of the Church has received renewed attention through the Pauline image of the Church as the body of Christ, of which he is the head and the members are the various parts and organs functioning in a vital union with him. St. Paul used this concept to emphasize both variety of function and equality of status and dignity, and this gives a modern relevance to this image. Finally, the community model of the Church in which the Church is viewed as the people of God is the most important of the new emphases of church life adopted in the Vatican Council. Its scriptural roots go back into early Jewish tradition; in an ecumenical age, this provides a strong authenticity for the model. From the viewpoint of the sociologist, this model suggests elements of structural flexibility, of communal sharing, of a wide identification with the aims and ideals of the group, of a use of authority in which the leader feels responsible to the members of the community. There is a feeling throughout the

Roman Catholic church today that, if the Church is the gathered people of God, a fellowship of those who believe and love, its members must study the nature and dynamics of social groups and adopt those styles and structures which make for positive growth and development.

This interest came home to me recently. I came across a local pastor who previously would have gathered his sociology from a mixture of papal encyclicals and *Time* magazine; he was busy reading *The Dynamics of Planned Change* by Lippitt, Watson and Westley. He commented to me that since he was now required to be a different kind of leader, responsible for initiating change in his parish, he felt that he had better find out what it was all about. He was interested in getting all his people to share in the tasks of goal definition, and of the clarification of community roles and functions. He saw the need of task forces and action groups to define issues and problems, and felt that he must promote the growth of new structures for the sharing of decisions and an increase in mutual responsiveness. He added, "all of this is implied in what they said at the council. Some of the students in the parish have been talking this over with me, and I'm lucky enough to have a friend who is a sociologist—he's been explaining it all to me, and he gave me this to read." This parish had an elected parish council which was a genuine expression of community responsibility, and a number of working groups in various fields of charity, education, worship, role definition and parish management which kept the parish council busy and active. Parishes of this type are still a tiny minority, but they point in a direction which church communities may take as the suggestions of the sociologists are discussed and absorbed.

With all this has come an increasing dissatisfaction with the sociological background and insights of many of the official statements of popes and bishops. "Encyclical sociology" has come in for increasing criticism for its outdated basic assumptions and concepts, its sweeping universalist judgments of social situations, and its tone of paternal admonition to modern scholarship. General notions such as "the principle of subsidiarity" are often used as simplistic, essentialist standards; this is in poor contrast with the careful analysis made by many sociologists of the relative values and optimum use of local responsibility and centralized organs.

Study of the function of the bureaucrat suggests that the linking of authority with function instead of with hierarchic position frees the bureaucrat from many of his impersonal roles. He should be free to develop more authentic roles in terms of research, wider planning, the fixing of operational standards, a genuine concern with personnel issues and problems, and the building of both horizontal and vertical lines of communication. Much study has been done of the relative value of individual work, small group work and centrally directed work in such areas as creativity, problem-solving, decision-making and planning-implementation. In these areas we may expect, from the dialog between Church and sociology, a greater sophistication in clarifying many of the present ambiguities in Catholic roles and structures. From the viewpoint of the priest, who has much to gain from this clarification, it is highly desirable that much of the energy at present being expended in authority conflict, anxiety, hostility and admonition should be transferred to these positive objectives.

This would involve the church community at all levels in a commitment to sociological study, research and discussion far beyond that of the present. In the meantime, while many new ideas and suggestions struggle for survival within the Church, the chief hope is in the strength of modern criticism and the open discussion which it leads to. These discussions range far beyond the Church's preoccupation with its internal structures. Eagleton comments on the historical background of Catholic weakness in areas of social commentary, and concludes:

The tepid liberalism of a good deal of the social criticism which has sprung from the catholic renewal of the sixties, the continuing distrust of detailed programme and of institution, the use of terms like "exploratory" and "open-ended" to rationalize a basic refusal of commitment—these can be seen as particular legacies from the past. The inability to think and feel beyond paternalistic and family models of community, in discussion both of church and community, the preoccupation with concrete and personal activity at the expense of more complex sociological thinking, are parts of the same inheritance.[2]

THE PRIEST'S ENCOUNTER WITH PSYCHOLOGY

Allied with sociology and group psychology in influencing the evolution of the priest's authority role are personality psychology and counseling. As we saw in the beginning of this book, many priests have turned to these areas of study as a result of their own role uncertainty and a lack of confidence in their traditional skills of advice and guidance. Particularly in the areas of adolescent and marriage counseling, priests have generally felt that their seminary training was inadequate. Fichter, in his study of priests and selected parishioners, asked the priests to rate a list of nine tasks as to which were most time-consuming and also as to which they were best prepared. Counseling people was rated as most time-consuming, followed by directing organizations, and by financial administration. Counseling was rated only third in terms of the training received, directing organizations was rated eighth, and financial administration was rated ninth.[3] Counseling and directing organizations would cover the great part of the priest's more serious dealings with his people, and it seems that in this area he feels the need for additional knowledge and skills from personal and group psychology. It is evident also that a better skill in community organiza-

[2] Terence Eagleton, *Catholics and the Left* (London: Sheed and Ward, 1966) , p. 81.
[3] Joseph H. Fichter, *Priest and People* (New York: Sheed and Ward, 1965) , p. 186.

tion may help him to deal more efficiently with problems of financial administration.

Catholic priests throughout our society are responding to this felt need by a notably increasing interest in personality psychology and counseling theory and practice. Comparatively large numbers of priests have gained, in recent years, a professional education and competence in these areas. Much larger numbers have taken part in seminars and extension courses. An expanding literature on pastoral counseling is promoting this general development. To the professionally respectable books of such Protestant counselors as Seward Hiltner have been added the competent writings of such Catholic priests as Curran, Godin, Hagmaier and Kennedy. This increasing enthusiasm of the clergy, stemming originally from the need to clarify their role and improve their technique, leads them into a familiarity with basic psychological concepts which in turn have a dynamic influence on their authority and leadership function.

Priests entering this field of study become aware of the wide persistence of infantile attitudes in religious behavior. They receive constant warnings from their lecturers, supervisors and authors about the way in which the dominating priest, even when he is kindly and fatherly, can be reinforcing his client in immature and infantile attitudes. Godin gives a typical warning:

> care must be taken in prolonged pastoral guidance not to induce in the counselee a sense of dependence or passivity in the making of decisions which would result in a total alienation of his moral consciousness and might well stunt his religious growth. This is a particularly pronounced risk in the case of pastors with dominating, authoritative, or pseudopaternal inclinations. As if by chance, they will see a crowd of anxious faces circling around them, the scrupulous and the weak who ask nothing better than a chance to shed before God the burden of normal responsibility which is the lot of every psychologically mature adult.[4]

[4] André Godin, *The Pastor as Counselor* (New York: Holt, Rinehart and Winston, 1965), pp. 46–47.

Repeated warnings of this kind throw into severe doubt many of the traditional images of the priest as a moral authority, a father who guards his spiritual children, a "spiritual director" who shows his clients the way of the Lord.

Priests who are open to this kind of study and competence become aware, also, of the tendency to absolutize various elements of our knowledge or experience into forms of intellectual and emotional narrowness. They become conscious that much of what has passed for a strict and loyal observance of religion has been, in fact, a kind of anxious legalism and narrow dogmatism. This more critical frame of thinking among the clergy makes them aware of the dangers of trying to legislate people into holiness, and rather suspicious of the kind of religious statement which begins with, "the only solution to all the troubles of the modern world is . . ."; or "every loyal Catholic must faithfully believe that. . . ." The practice of psychology and counseling presents a strong demand for a broad and open mind, a deep respect for others and for their present stage of religious and emotional growth, and a warm and welcoming acceptance of persons regardless of their opinions and behavior. As these basic attitudes become more accepted and normal among the clergy, a very significant evolution is under way in their own role concept.

Psychology leads the priest in the positive direction of searching for the maturity of his own growth, and of building church structures which will favor the growth of maturity in others. The studies of the personality psychologists lead him into the area of the practical conditions of human growth and its expression in warm, secure and relaxed interpersonal relationships; they involve him in a search for personal and group creativity, self actualization, a realistic life view and a personalized religious orientation. The priest may find in the lives of these psychologists, in their clinical work and case notes, and in their group work, a model of leadership which seems to be very effective while being relaxed and unobtrusive. This leadership is aimed directly at the growth and maturity of the client or group; it is seen as successful when it results in a mature acceptance of responsibility, of self-decision, and of personal integration of life with all its inconsistencies and contradictions.

Rogers gives a brief summary of this relationship:

> we have found that the therapist is most effective if he is: (a) genuine, integrated, transparently real in the relationship; (b) acceptant of the client as a separate, different, person, and acceptant of each fluctuating aspect of the client as it comes to expression; and (c) sensitively empathic in his understanding, seeing the world through the client's eyes.[5]

He goes on to describe the predictable consequences in the client: "the client will become more self-directing, less rigid, more open to the evidence of his senses, better organized and integrated, more similar to the ideal which he has chosen for himself." [6]

This kind of relationship, which increasing numbers of priests are now entering into, is already providing a working model for the clergy as they search for a new interpretation of the New Testament ideal of authority as a form of loving service in brotherly equality. It is having its effect also in helping priests to accept more easily their changing role and all the discontinuities and conflicts which mark this period of its evolution.

The enthusiasm of some of the clergy in embracing psychology as a solution to their role confusions and to the problems of the Church has merited many warnings from psychologists, who see in this a danger of a new absolutism which their own tentative conclusions will not bear. I have myself had to deal with the problems of priests, who, often without realizing it, have in effect resigned from their ministry to become amateur psychologists; they seem to have built around their new learning a secu-

---

[5] Carl Rogers, *On Becoming a Person* (Boston: Houghton Mifflin Co., 1961), p. 397.
[6] *Loc. cit.*

rity system which will not bear the weight of their anxieties. Educated as they have been in a highly dogmatized and essentialist theological system, they have tended to make their psychology into a new dogmatism which ends up far away from the fluidity and flexibility of the mature psychologist. This danger seen in individual priests is also an evident danger within the Church as a whole, and for much the same reasons. If the role of the priest in the future is not to be fossilized within a new set of modern-sounding rigidities, priests must be searching for a deeper perception of what the best of psychology has to offer, and must take note of its limitations and its warnings.

Erikson issues such a warning in an analysis he makes of law and child-training, and their relationship to social institutions:

> The dependence of any institution on rejuvenation by the emotional investment of generations brings with it a persistent double danger. Even as the individual, in frantic search of his earliest hope-giving relationship, may end up lost in delusions and addictions, so are religions, when they lose their bonds with living ethics, apt to regress to the fostering of illusory and addictive promises of empty fantasy. And even as the individual, under the impact of his infantile training in domestic law and order, can become "compulsive," i.e., excessively controlled by and concerned with the mechanisms of inner control, so organized law can become machinery using the letter to subdue the spirit which was to be safeguarded. One can speak, then, of "sick" institutions, but only as long as one specifies the adaptive mechanisms which have bogged down in mere repetitiveness; and as long as one does not indulge in the assumption that psychiatric enlightenment as such will heal society.[7]

SOME EMERGING STRUCTURES

It is, then, with a critical view that we look at the part new church structures are playing in the reshaping of the role of the priest. While new structures allowing for open elections of parish councils, councils of the clergy of a diocese, and even of bishops are tentatively emerging within the Church since the Vati-

[7] Erik H. Erikson, *Insight and Responsibility* (New York: Norton, 1964), p. 155.

can Council, there is present a double danger as far as the priest's role is concerned. In the first place these can easily develop into a pleasant style of group exercise without any basic shift in the power structure. For example, a pastor or bishop enthusiastically sets up all the new structures suggested by the Vatican Council or by friendly sociologists; he allows them to work freely and to make many minor decisions even against his opinion, but all the decisions which he considers important are still really made by himself. This authority style is part of the expertise of experienced administrators and politicians, and is merely a sophisticated form of the liberal paternalism which Eagleton speaks of. This kind of structural renewal, already widely in existence within the Church, can lead only to new ambiguities and frustrations for the priest. Already there are wide feelings within the Church that the high ideals of group-sharing and equality outlined in the council documents are somewhat illusory in their promises. This is the danger which Erikson called "the fostering of illusory and addictive promises of empty fantasy."

The second danger to the priest's role in the new structures is that they may easily become fixed in a new rigidity by a whole series of norms, directives and regulations, and so, again, betray their original promise. I have been in many discussions with priests on the subject of priests' associations and elected councils. In many of these discussions, the whole value of flexibility and adaptiveness seemed in danger of being lost in an enthusiasm for legal constitutions and regulations. The new legalisms, it seemed to me, would end up being as narrow and confining as the old ones which they were so enthusiastically replacing. It seemed very difficult for many priests to see the possibility of a group life which emphasized freedom, creativity, the authority of a working function, and a security based on respect for persons and their individual differences. Here is Erikson's second danger in action: when he spoke of organized law becoming a machinery using the letter to subdue the spirit which was to be safeguarded.

With, then, these cautions against wide-eyed wonder, it is possible to view these emerging structures as an important part of the evolution of a new working role for the Catholic priest. Particularly if they are not isolated in their effect by an adherence to personal attitudes of paternalism and submissiveness more appropriate to the former structures, they could play an important part in the shaping of a new set of priestly functions. For example, in a parish council elected by the local Christian brotherhood to share responsibility and leadership with the priest in areas of Christian teaching, worship, community concern, social welfare, problems of morality and parish management, the priest may find for himself a new kind of leadership; he may find his meaning as servant and minister of the gospel through working in terms of functional equality and a respect for mutual dignity and competence.

A priest who is working in this direction with his parishioners remarked to me recently that so far he found his new role personally challenging, satisfying and authentically human. He said, "I seem now to be more a man amongst men than a distant figure or symbol." He went on to suggest that as Maslow had seen his mature persons as self-actualizing, he thought that his parish group, too, should be self-actualizing; it was his task to help people to be open to the energies inherent within their Christian fellowship, and to help them see the New Testament ideal of life, love and truth as their challenge. "To me," he commented, "it's like a good friendship. In a friendship you become more your real self, not less, through being open to another; and in a friendship you actually have much more influence, and, if you like, real authority, precisely because you are a genuine friend and not a symbol of some legalism. For example, I really have much more influence over you than does any policeman or bishop." This priest, typically and properly, is still relating his new experience to past formulations of his role. If his search with his people goes on in the building of new relationships and the finding of new securities, this need may easily disappear. The point here is that he is even at present finding all of this satisfying, more deeply human and more authentically religious.

This seems to me to be a personal example of what Eagleton is stressing in his study of relationships and structures in the Church. He emphasizes that those who think all that is required is a change of consciousness so that everyone would feel equal are making a typical liberal mistake. Structures create their own attitudes, so a reform of structures is equally important with the change of personal attitudes. Eagleton writes:

> the full, revolutionary meaning of common responsibility has not been grasped. The confusion at the root of this is the confusion between function and relationship; certain functions, certain roles and skills within society, have become traditionally associated with a whole superstructure of relationship, which is then institutionalized in terms of authority or paternalism or service. The movement towards common responsibility is the movement to return to this sense of role and skill, without its context of social inequality.[8]

The extent of the change already under way in structures of church life is not generally recognized. If these are not to outdistance the change in attitudes and die of a creeping paternalism, it is necessary that they should be openly discussed and evaluated in terms of attitudes to authority and leadership. For example, the Vatican Council recommends the setting up of church councils at the parish level and the level of the diocese; in speaking of their functions, it uses rather indeterminate words such as participate, advise, and dialog. In many sections, as we have seen, there is a strong emphasis on the authority of bishops. Here is an area already fruitful in misunderstanding and frustration, and in which priests are rightly confused about their changing role. Are they meant to share a common responsibility with their parishioners in the way we have just de-

8 Terence Eagleton, *The New Left Church* (Baltimore: Helicon, 1966), p. 109.

scribed, or are parish councils strictly advisory bodies, with the priests and bishops still making all the important decisions?

Many committees of lay people appointed to areas of diocesan responsibility, such as social welfare, marriage guidance, the governing of seminaries and colleges, and the administration of school systems, are facing the same questions. In this early period of development there is a great determination that the new bodies, so much in the public eye, should work well and effectively. Much of what is lacking in clarity of structure and role is being made up for by earnest goodwill. Once the time of novelty is past, there may be many collisions of interest unless attention is paid to the kind of flexible, evolving structure which is needed to support these ventures.

One of the more promising signs is an emerging interest in social structure and sociology on the part of professional theologians. More of them are seeing that their theories must be related to the ongoing reality of human development if they are to be viable. An excellent example of this is seen in McKenzie's study of church authority, from which we have quoted; he shows himself willing to test his scriptural scholarship and theological insight against the reality of our present human situation. Another distinguished example of this tendency is Karl Rahner, who, in discussing the theological implications of a council of world bishops working with the Pope, comments:

> Today it is in practice scarcely possible to make sure that the ruler of a large community (society) with manifold tasks in extremely complicated conditions is well-informed unless he is aided by a team-government, brains-trust, or something of the kind, even if he alone has the last word. The idea that, even today, a well-educated man with good intentions and great personal "experience" can be sufficiently well-informed without more ado and without the need of institutionalized information facilities, is old Frankish paternalism which has nothing to do with the juridical freedom and independence of a supreme ruler.[9]

[9] Karl Rahner, *Bishops: Their Status and Function* (Baltimore: Helicon, 1963) , p. 70.

While this style of writing shows the ambiguities which underlie much of the role confusion in the Church, it is an important advance in bringing theology into a tardy relation with social reality.

A further important area of renewal is the increased interest in legal process within the Church, particularly in the case of appeals against authoritative and administrative decisions. It is known that this is receiving the attention of the canon lawyers in their reform of the whole legal system of the Church. Some particular attention and interest has focused on the ombudsman function, characteristic of Scandinavian society. This is a publicly appointed officer who receives complaints against decisions and investigates them fully. Archbishop Roberts, in a submission to the Vatican Council in 1963, quoted the value of ombudsmen, as seen in such "socially advanced areas" as the Scandinavian countries and New Zealand, and urged that provision should be made for them in church life. In an article reporting on the New Zealand experience (in *America* magazine, January 30, 1965), I pointed out that the ombudsman is given no direct authority over the matter of citizens' complaints; he is instead given full power of investigation, with access to documents, reports and files, and has authority to make his findings public. I commented:

> The Ombudsman cannot himself rectify complaints when he thinks they are justified; he merely reports his recommendations to the head of the department concerned. If he is not satisfied with the department's reply, he may report the matter to the Prime Minister or directly to Parliament. In any case, as an officer of Parliament, he must submit an annual report. These reports are available to the press and to any citizen.[10]

The New Zealand ombudsman has found that only a small proportion of complaints are justified on investigation, and that his recommendations in these cases are generally followed by the

[10] David P. O'Neill, "The New Zealand Ombudsman," in *America*, vol. 112, no. 5 (January 30, 1965), p. 166.

departments concerned. He points, in his annual reports, to aspects of administrative process which generate complaints, and the most important effect of his work has been the general improvement and humanizing of bureaucratic procedure, and a greater openness on the part of bureaucrats to listen carefully to difficulties and complaints. I have found a widespread interest in this social institution within church circles, and a study of this function is going on at present in several dioceses. It has, for church life at the moment, the useful effect of improving administration and communication without being legally cumbersome and without demanding any immediate change in accepted lines of authority.

RADICAL THINKING WITHIN THE CHURCH

Christianity in its early days was considered by the conservative authorities of Judaism and of the Roman Empire as a dangerous movement of radicals; many modern commentators have discussed the strong radical quality about the discipleship of the early Christians. This quality became institutionalized in the monastic movement, allowing a more easy conformity for the general body of the faithful and their hierarchic leaders. This provided for much mutual interaction through the legalizing of monasticism and through the emergence of occasional charismatic figures from the monastery into the wider community. However, the balance between the hierarchic Church and its prophetic, charismatic figures has usually remained an uneasy one. In a large proportion of cases, the prophet with his charismatic gifts and revolutionary attitudes has left the union of the Church, or has been expelled, and has formed a new group of radical Christians. The new group, in turn, tends to institutionalize these gifts and attitudes into a new orthodoxy, which may end up surprisingly similar to the one from which they sprang.

There is, within the Church at present, a strong opinion that now, with improved communication and human understanding, it should be possible to unite these separated elements of church life more functionally. Radical voices within the Church, and within other Christian churches, are being listened to by a wider audience and with greater toleration. Through books, newsmagazines and television, the radical thinker now has a much wider intelligent audience. He has, too, the safeguard of public opinion against the traditional methods which the hierarchy have used to silence him or expel him from the church community. This has an important generalized effect on the priest and his role, particularly in its effect of promoting change more quickly and securely. It points, also, to a shift of power within the Church away from the traditional lines of authority into the area of community responsibility and public consent; this has the effect of a change of role for the priest in his middle position between bishop and people.

While in the United States in 1966, I had a long discussion on this topic with a sociologist who was teaching in one of the church universities. "Power within the church community has already moved away from the bishops," he told me; "many of them do not seem to be conscious of the fact that autocratic decisions are, in many cases, no longer within their power as public leaders. Through modern communication, public opinion, both within the Church and in the wider community, now exercises a balancing power which often overrules the traditional power of the bishop." He instanced the case of the Jesuit theologian and social actionist, Daniel Berrigan. His church superiors quietly and quickly ordered him to South America, in a fairly obvious attempt to remove him from the North American scene, and from his concern with the peace movement. While he obeyed dutifully, his friends were joined by thousands of Catholics, including priests, nuns and seminarians, in a wave of public protest that resulted in Berrigan's recall to New York with freedom to continue his teaching and practice of radical Christianity.

Cases of this kind have been frequent in the United States during the past few years, suggesting that bishops and other church authorities are finding difficulty in adjusting to their new role of being leaders responsible to an articulate community. While I am writing, the case of Charles Curran, a mildly radical theology professor, has just been concluded after headlines around the world. The board of bishops who controlled Catholic University in Washington decided quietly not to renew his contract to teach. When faced by a strike of students and faculty in the university, and an overwhelming vote of public opinion against them on the ground of academic freedom and due process, the bishops were forced to reverse their decision and to rehire Curran with due promotion.

The consequent fear of many church authorities has been expressed in innumerable warnings, cautions and appeals to the clergy for loyalty and obedience. Many priests have told me that they feel that these loyalty appeals are reactionary; they are a harking back to a social situation that has disappeared for good, and mark a continuing refusal to study the new situation and the attitudes and structures it demands. Meantime, from some of the radical thinkers, who are often capable of a more objective view, comes a warning against an easy acceptance of a movement of power within the Church. Harvey Cox, in an article entitled "Revolt in the Church," warns that lay people who gain control of church activity can be as narrowly conservative in social policy as any board of bishops. He states:

> Protestants in America have not been troubled recently by excessive clerical control over their activities in the secular realm. The battle, therefore, is in no sense a battle for the freedom of laymen and activist clergy against a dominating hierarchy. In Protestantism, activist ministers must often contend with the socially conservative laymen who sit on the boards that rule the churches. This is particularly interesting in view of the vocal demands among Catholic lay-

men today for a wider responsibility in the governance of their church. Protestantism in America, at least in its main-line denominations, is far from being completely lay controlled, but it is often where lay control is most powerful that the opposition to social action has been most vociferous.[11]

This warning highlights the value of the constructive thinking from the viewpoints of sociology, psychology and practical structure-building, which is going on quietly in many areas of the Church. Many of these thinkers and planners are already quoted in this book; they see the need in terms of real social evolution, of a change in interpersonal attitudes and relationships and a corresponding change in group structures. These two dynamic elements in a changing institution are mutually supportive and necessary. This emphasis, so notably missing in the documents of the Vatican Council, is well explained in the manifesto of the English Slant group, entitled *Catholics and the Left*. This is a moderate statement of radical Christianity for our time, with a sober consideration of the factors we have outlined in this chapter. In this group, and particularly in Eagleton's writing, we find an honest attempt to study the nature and style of a free and self-determining church group, to consider the attitudes and structures it needs, and the kind of social stance which might make it meaningful to its members and to the wider community.

On the side of the theologians, we expect too much if we look for the same social sophistication; few of them are socially involved, and few could be called radical in any real sense. Radical Catholics find their speculations timid when it comes to the point of practical programing. This is in strong contrast with Protestant theologians of the type of Harvey Cox, who does not hesitate to follow up his radical thinking with a discussion of the type of social involvement his thinking leads to. We have commented previously on the tendency among Catholic thinkers

[11] Harvey Cox, "Revolt in the Church," in *Playboy*, January, 1967, p. 209.

to avoid major issues of difficulty and tension and to concentrate attention on safer areas and minor issues. A perusal of Catholic theological journals, such as *Concilium, Theology Digest, Worship* and *Bible Today,* seems to justify this criticism. By this kind of unwitting collusion we have described, there is a concentration on conflict-free issues and safe intellectual arguments. When a moderate piece of orthodox theological speculation comes from someone like Harvey Cox or the Slant group who follow theology into its real life implications, it seems to Catholics to be either a new revelation or to be wildly heretical. A good deal of this is a difficulty in communications, as we shall see in the next chapter. Here it is sufficient to emphasize that, because of this situation, the impact of the new radical writing on the clergy is much greater than should normally be the case. While these new and tentative ventures in practical theology are certainly disturbing and confusing for many priests, they form a very important intellectual background of the evolution of the priest's role and authority function.

THE STRAINS OF FREEDOM

We have seen, in the chapters on freedom and the new morality, that each new development in the life of the priest brings with it its new problems, conflicts and role confusion. This consideration of the current developments in the authority-functioning of the priest is no exception. Here is a continuing situation that is full of ambiguities, a situation in which priests continue to function even while most of them are not very sure where they stand on any number of these basic issues. The greater part of the ancient authority system of the Church stands on one side of a hardly visible, highly elusive, and constantly shifting dividing line that marks off a generally traditionalist set of attitudes and values. Many priests, for whatever psychological, religious or social reasons, stay firmly on the right side of this line. On the other side of the line are a bewildering variety of people: a few bishops and theologians, a substantial proportion of the clergy, and large numbers of lay people. As we have seen, they represent a variety of attitudes and opinions, from a mild liberalism to a deeply committed radicalism.

Perhaps the largest group of priests stand, rather uneasily, with one foot on either side of the line, if they can find out just where it is at the moment. Here they hope to be able to listen to the loyalty appeals and warnings from Pope and bishop without too much anxiety of conscience, and to be able to mix with their liberal and radical friends with reasonable caution and with the considerable satisfaction of knowing that they are on the side that will win out eventually. Whatever position the priest takes, whether in a fixed or in a flexible attitude, whether in one extreme or the other, or in some situation of compromise, whether in an intellectual synthesis or in a refusal to think about it at all, he is likely to be affected deeply by problems of personal and social identity, and by the current doubts, confusions and conflicts concerning the role which is his life commitment.

Some of the typical anguish of this situation can be felt in the comments of Charles Davis, the English theologian who resigned from the Church in 1966. Some months before his resignation, he wrote in an editorial an analysis of the present relationship between clergy and laity, stressing that lay people are widely rejecting the traditional paternalism of the priest in both its aspects of authority and communication. Speaking of the varying attitudes of the clergy, he mentioned the lack of correspondence between the close personal relationships that many priests have with lay people and the institutional structures under which both still live in the Church. He added:

> The slowness of existing structures to change is in fact having a noteworthy effect. Increasingly the Christian activity of reflective and earnest lay people is being carried on outside those structures or with only a nominal connexion with them. Catholics are meeting, discussing and acting together in informal groups, while having

little outside the liturgy to do with the formal organization of the church. They look to sympathetic priests for support. . . .[12]

He points out that in general this is a very healthy development, but poses the question,

> Is it healthy that this development should be accompanied by a despairing sense that the formal structure of the church is beyond bothering about? To ignore the formal structure of the church implies an inadequate grasp of the visible reality of the church as a community. In particular it leaves priests in a very unsatisfactory position. Inevitably their life is closely determined by the ecclesiastical set-up. Whatever their informal contacts, the proper fulfilment of their role as priests is grounded upon a satisfactory relationship with the laity within the formal structure of the church. Otherwise their role remains unclear, and the more they are with the laity the more their life is divided into two unco-ordinated segments.[13]

The dichotomy of the priest's role conflict is a shifting one. It has been, no doubt, experienced variously in different periods of the Church's history, and in different geographic and cultural situations. We have seen, in the course of this book, many different viewpoints on this conflict in the present day, more particularly in the English-speaking areas. There are signs, as we shall see in the remaining chapters, that the argument is moving rapidly to new positions, and is beginning to center around new syntheses of priestly function and role. Since the underlying element in these new discussions seems to be the area of communication and its meaning within the Church, this is our next topic for discussion.

[12] From an editorial in *The Clergy Review*, July, 1966, Charles Davis, editor.
[13] *Ibid.*

8:BEING THE MIDDLE-MAN IN THE NET /
communications and meaning

Most students of the modern Church, if asked to name the least significant statements of the Vatican Council, would be likely to nominate the _Decree on Communications_, closely followed by the _Declaration on Christian Education_. From what we have seen in this book so far there is a certain irony in the body of Catholic bishops teaching the world on these topics; it seems that precisely on these subjects the bishops were least open to new and critical ideas. It is not surprising that these ingroup statements base themselves on rather outmoded social stances, and come to many conclusions that are rejected by large numbers of priests and lay people in the Church, as well as by the general educated opinion of our societies. For example, large numbers of Catholics have in discussion with me found it unbelievable that the bishops, in the second chapter of the communications document, have recommended them to patronize movie theaters managed by upright Catholics, to encourage Catholic features on television, and to join in efforts to establish Catholic television stations. This kind of social separatism characterizes both these documents; it runs counter to an increasing trend in Catholic thinking which demands an open dialog and involvement with the affairs and concerns of the wider social community, and a far greater openness in the Church's internal and external communications. As we search for the shape of the priest's role, this trend provides us with a clear direction.

From the viewpoint of the social sciences, we may see the Church precisely as a communications system. The familiar scriptural images and symbols point in this direction; God speaks to his people, the people have a spokesman before the Lord, the Lord sends prophets to give forth his message, sends his son who comes to be called the Word of God, and chooses a group of followers whom he calls apostles or messengers. The Christian Church is a fellowship of those who hear the message, who listen to God and to one another in mutual love and care. As we saw when speaking of new moral trends, the Christian is one who is in dialog with God and with men, one who orients his life as a "Yes" to God's call to love. The worship of the Church is a group affirmation of this life orientation, a people listening to God and making a united response of dedication and sharing.

In this view, an interest in modern communication is not a kind of optional extra for the Church, for communication is the mode of its being. It is not something that can be expressed in an enthusiasm for Catholic newspapers, television stations, movie theaters, radio networks, school systems and universities, all under the watchful eye of bishops, but rather something the very opposite. These Catholic structures depend on a view of the Church as a group basically separate from the general society of men, over against the rest of mankind, setting up a separate system of communication to speak to its own members and to give out a message to the rest of men. The view we are considering sees the Church as a communication system within the whole community of man. In this view the Church belongs to everyone, and is common property serving the whole community like a telephone system or a set of communication satellites.

Once again we sense a basic dichotomy which is of deep relevance for the role of the priest. This relevance occurs not merely because the priest is caught up in the continuing argument about the value of parochial schools or Catholic universities. Much of the discussion on this topic, and much of the social research, seems to miss the point we are making. The question for the priest in his search for role, is not whether a parochial school helps his Catholic children to say their prayers better or to go to church more often, or even to take a Christian attitude to problems of race, poverty and peace. It is rather the question whether his school may not be a denial of the meaning of the Church as a system of communication for his whole social community. The Church, like a telephone system, is a community facility in the area of communication and should have its links with the whole community.

This view of the Church in terms of communications presents the priest, as a religious functionary, with the question of whether there can be any authentic role for him in one of a group of competing Christian churches. It also raises the more basic question of whether the Church, even if it were united, can continue to have the social shape of a community within a community. This social form may well come to be seen as a direct denial of what Christianity seeks to affirm.

The priest's role is still strongly centered around the internal needs and services of the Church as a distinct community. The internal religious and social needs of Catholics are still his primary concern. There is an idea that if these needs are well catered for, Catholics will bear witness to the rest of men in a dedicated and convincing way. What does come through as a message to the rest of men is the whole social shape of this effort; Catholics are seen as a separated group, rather odd in their ways, who still manage to do quite a deal of good at times. To join them seems like joining a rather quaintly exclusive brotherhood with many internal benefits, and quite a few disadvantages.

It seems that the very social shape which the Church has taken is a stronger and clearer communication than its authentic message to man. This message seeks to enter into dialog with all men at the level of ultimate meaning: that level where man asks his perennial questions about meaning and destiny, about life and death, about truth and love, about good and evil, about darkness and light. The Church is a message saying that in this tradition, in these scriptures, in this person of Christ, God is speaking to man about life and destiny, truth and love. The priest is the middleman, the mediator; his task is to mediate this message, to proclaim this good news to man.

Many priests will see this as an oversimple view which fails to take into account how very complex is the present church situation in terms of its religious, social and historical evolution. However this may be, it is a view which is commanding the increasing attention of students of the Church from many viewpoints, and underlies a good deal of modern popular discussion of religion. It seems to me, from my discussions of the priest role with all kinds of groups, that this is one of the ground questions of the discussion. Because it is such a disturbing question, it tends to bring into play the rationalizations, defences and anxieties we have discussed in this book. Examples of this can be seen in much of the Catholic response to such books as Mary Perkins Ryan's treatment of parochial schools, Harvey Cox's view of the secular city, and the writing of the theologians who speak of religionless Christianity. While these studies have started much intelligent comment and research among Catholics, the highly emotional character of much of the response shows how deeply the basic issue we have outlined affects the identity and security of the present Catholic community. This issue also throws into strong relief the importance of much of the current discussion on the functioning of communications within the Church.

ABOUT HUMAN COMMUNICATIONS

The word "communication" is being used in many senses at present, all of which are interrelated. We speak in this section of communication between persons, as studied by psychologists and sociologists. We shall look later at communication theory in terms of systems, which by improving in a few aspects on the human model, are providing our world with a new reach into reality and with a new technology.

Human communication can be described as a mutual sharing of information—facts, ideas, feelings, opinions, plans and theories —with a view to common decision and common action. We can use this concept for communication between two, as in a marriage, between members of a small group, between the members of a social institution such as the Church is at present, or between the members of a whole society. Our definition inevitably fails to register the variety and complexity of human communication and the deeper dimensions of interpersonal dynamics; however, it is short and simple enough for us to begin discussion. This concept is useful also in personality psychology when we consider the dialog which every person carries on within himself, as he says, "Who am I—what am I going to do—what is happening in me—is this really what I am like—" and so on. It is important, for good personal, interpersonal and social functioning that our lines of communication should be free and open, and reasonably clear of major blocks and distortions. When this is not so, elements of unreality can have a snowballing effect leading to various forms of human misery and breakdown. Let us then expand our initial concept a little by looking at the main functions of human communication.

Through good communication we become aware of ourselves and others as persons: we are, and we listen, and we respond, and we find out who we are and who is the other. One of the first casualties of faulty communication is our sense of identity and our secure perception of the person and meaning of others. Through the whole net of human communication within which we live and grow, we are becoming, ideally, more fully ourselves and more fully human, as others are doing through their life with us. By some paradox, it is in our identification with others in this mutual sharing that we find the full meaning of ourselves. When we withdraw ourselves, and try to live outside this net of communications, we become less ourselves, we become less authentic as persons, we gain a feeling of being lost, of being isolated. It is interesting to remember that isolated and insulated both come from the Latin root word for an island. John Donne beautifully expressed this in his *Meditation 17:* "No man is an island, entire of itself; every man is a piece of the continent, a part of the main . . . any man's death diminishes me, because I am involved in mankind; and therefore never send to know for whom the bell tolls; it tolls for thee."

Through this open interaction of persons, and the free flow of information—facts and theories, ideas and emotions, insights and plans—which good communications provide for, we are able mutually to define goals and directions for our common life. We become aware of roles and functions, of courtesies and rituals and symbols. We are able to enter into discussion of practical plans, to act together, to criticize our results, and to learn from experience. In the sense that the Church is a sharing fellowship, this is its mode of existence; as the priest is some kind of middleman in the Church, he is a centerpoint in a communications net, with the function of keeping the channels open, and of providing for the free flow of information and response.

A great deal of study is being done in our time on faulty communication, on the way in which persons, in their inner dialog with themselves, and in their relationships with others, find their communication blocked or distorted. The whole work of therapeutic psychologists and counselors deals with this area of faulty communication, as does, at another level, that of the social worker and the social change agent. Because the function of these professionals is generally to open up the channels of communication and to promote the healthy interchange in which the growth we have described may develop, some priests have seen in this area a model for the kind of work they should do as mediators in the Church. We shall discuss this suggestion in the final chapter.

Communication deals with conflict; in fact, conflict is itself a kind of communication. Human conflict is not only inevitable, it is essential. Basically, it is a recognition of human difference, of human uniqueness, of the simple fact that not all people think alike, feel alike, plan alike, or want to act in the same way. These differences are sharpened by feeling and emotion into conflict, argument, discussion. An essential part of every form of human communication, then, is its style of dealing with conflict. Some forms tend to deny that conflict exists; this is the most destructive misuse of communication, and one which tends to exist in many family situations, particularly in higher income groups. Other faulty styles of communication recognize conflict, but deny its value through various styles of distorted perception, through patterned attitudes of paternalism and submissiveness, and through multiple ignorance. A wide variety of fears and anxieties may distort the meaning of conflict; they tend to destroy its interpersonal value and its positive role in the defining of goals and plans and in the affirming of human dignity and identity.

A major task, then, of all systems of human communication is to exercise that degree of social control over conflict that keeps aggressiveness and defensiveness below the destructive level, so that the energies generated from difference and conflict may become available for community goals. Most of our communities, therefore, institutionalize conflict in various ways: in law courts, in open elections of all kinds, in parliamentary systems, in town meetings, in discussion groups and debates, and, for the sick, in therapy groups of one kind or another. It is important to realize that we have found it useful to pay competent and highly selected men precisely to oppose the plans and decisions of government, the actions and conclusions of policemen, and the right to office of even highly respected politicians and statesmen; we regard this institutionalizing of conflict as one of the major social achievements of our western communities.

ABOUT SYSTEM COMMUNICATION

Cybernetics, of which we hear so much in this kind of discussion, comes from the Greek word for a man who steers a ship, a root which also gives us our words governor and gubernatorial. Generally, people use the word cybernetics to refer to systems of communication and control in machines. A machine is built to receive information, to process it in terms of its built-in programming, and either to release it in a form more useful to its human master, or to carry out some programmed task in which it may be self-steering and self-correcting. In this latter function, it gathers new information in the form of feedback as it progresses, and processes this into modified directions. This young field of human endeavor, fed with the skills, insight and data of electrical engineering, neurophysiology and mathematical logic, has not only leapt rapidly into many of the practical concerns of our life, it has enriched us with analogies and insights for many other fields, particularly that of human communication. Through the effort of studying the process of communication and control for the purpose of designing machines that work, men have come to understand this process much more clearly in human beings and human groups.

Karl Deutsch, as long ago as 1950, sought a unifying concept for these analogies in an essay entitled "Mechanism, Teleology, and Mind." He presents a concept which brings together for study human communication, both individual and social, and machine systems of communication. He spoke of a self-modifying communications network or learning net:

> Such a learning net would be any system characterized by a relevant degree of organization, communication, and control, regardless of the particular processes by which its messages are transmitted and its functions carried out—whether by words between individuals in a social organization, or by nerve cells and hormones in a living body, or by electric signals in an electronic device.[1]

Through this wider view of communication, it is possible to transfer the learnings of one field to another. From the field of electronic engineering it has been possible for the social scientist to gain a much sharper concept of the notion of information, feedback, message, self-steering, pathological learning, social efficiency, maximized abundance, and so on.

COMMUNICATION IN THE CHURCH

If, as we have suggested, the Church is a group whose special mode and purpose is human communication at a certain level of human meaning, it should be possible to evaluate its present operation in terms of the concepts and analogies discussed in the past few pages. This, clearly enough, would be a major project for some communications expert. We can take only a brief glance at the situation from the viewpoint of this book, that of the changing role of the priest within the Church. Almost every serious book I have read, these last few years, about the present condition of the Catholic church has noted the problem of poor, defective and outmoded communication within the Church, and from the Church to the human community. Many of the discussions and seminars I have taken part in with priests on their problems have circled round the same intractable difficulty. Let

---

[1] Karl W. Deutsch, "Mechanism, Teleology, and Mind," in *Space, Time and the New Mathematics,* Robert W. Marks, editor (New York: Bantam Books, 1964) , p. 227.

us look at three most frequently raised areas of concern: paternalism, secrecy and censorship.

Paternalism is a word which seems to be occurring in every chapter of this book. This is natural enough; it is one of those pervasive hierarchic attitudes, socially and theologically dysfunctional in our present development, which remains as a relic of the Church's past history. We have looked at many examples of it through this book, and shall see more in the next chapter or two. Here it is enough to emphasize again that its complementary attitude of submissiveness also remains widespread in the church community, not least among priests. Since the lives of priests and their general well-being is still so much in the hands of the bishops, this persisting attitude is not surprising. It does seem, with some of the structural developments described in the last chapter, that the opportunity has clearly arrived for both bishops and priests to replace these worn-out attitudes with those more appropriate to the newly emerging relationships.

In the meantime, priests and lay people experience the paternal attitude as a block in communication. So many of them, over the past few years, have worked at moderate and constructive proposals for church reform, only to hear them accepted with a few kind and fatherly words and with an assurance that the bishops are studying this matter already, or are waiting for some norms from Rome. In spite of all the warmth and geniality, the makers of the proposals feel that they are being treated like children, and that their work will not be seriously considered. The fatherly tone of most bishops' statements, and their admonitions to "our dear children in Christ" in the "name of our holy mother the Church," tend to promote the same feeling of frustration. The frequent calls for the kind of loyalty which leaves all decisions to the Pope or the bishop with a demand that there be no further public discussion, all of these lead to a massive block in communication within the Church. Since the tone of the Church's dealing with the wider community of men and with other church bodies is often equally patronizing, the flow of real information is likely to be blocked by some degree of frustration, resentment, and a general feeling that the Roman Catholic church has not, after all, changed very much.

Robert Marks, cyberneticist and social philosopher, commenting on the relevance of freedom in relation to the wealth explosion, makes a comment that fits this situation in the Church:

> Social repression, under whatever slogan, is social inefficiency, an inhibition of feedback, a disruption in the communications net. A self-steering system that blocks its own internal information, its capacity for the nursing of novelty and innovation, loses its ability to meet new situations successfully. It diminishes its intelligence. It foredooms its strivings towards attainable goals in a universe of change. And its end, like the societies of the Mayans and the Medes, is probable extinction. This is not a prophecy, but a probability statement. It is statistical mechanics applied to a social net.[2]

A cult of secrecy marks much of the administration of the Roman Catholic church. Generally, if there is any way of planning or of making decisions in a way which is secret rather than open, the secret way will be chosen. The overall effect of this is well described by Marks in the quotation above: group intelligence is ignored, and particularly the experience of the man-on-the-spot; the whole system shows small capacity for experiment and change. In case anyone might think that this book is attacking bishops too often, here is an opportunity to point out that these distorted attitudes pervade the Catholic organization at all levels. Bishops complain about the way in which the Pope and his curial assistants make decisions about local affairs without informing or consulting them. Priests have similar complaints about bishops, curates about pastors, and lay people complain about the priests. It seems that, in the vertically organized authority system of the Church, those in authority have a constant need to "keep them in their place," and "let them see who is

2 Robert W. Marks in *Space, Time and the New Mathematics*, Robert W. Marks, editor (New York: Bantam Books, 1964), p. 277.

really running the Church." Secrecy of plans and decisions performs the function of reinforcing authority. However, through the resentment it provokes, and the feeling of not being trusted, it occasions a blocking and distortion of the message received. As we have seen, upward communication is stifled in much the same way and for much the same reasons.

Spencer, an English sociologist, discusses in an article entitled "The Catholic Church and Communication" the style of the Church's communication in the period since the Reformation. After dealing with censorship in theology, he goes on:

> In matters non-theological the cult of secrecy prevailed at all levels from the Roman Curia to the city parish. This obsession choked communication processes. These suffered in any event from the obstacles usually found in a hierarchic structure. Downward communication of information was restricted in order to keep inferiors in their place and prevent unwanted initiatives. Upward communication was distorted by the desire to please the superior. Lateral communication was minimized, partly because of the jealousies found between equals in the hierarchic system, and partly because of the ideological stress on the vertical relationship. Finally, the content of the communication reflected technical weaknesses in the system for collecting information. Formal reporting was required for the purpose of enforcing discipline, not for collecting objective facts.[3]

Spencer goes on to discuss the change wrought by the Vatican Council in this established situation, and some of the tensions it is generating. It seems to me that the council, although its statements are ambiguous, stressing both change and hierarchic lines of authority, has generated a movement towards openness and free communication; but those in authority positions at all levels seem to be anxious and confused as they try to cope with a new situation without benefit of tradition or personal experience. There is, in consequence, a good deal of withdrawal into old attitudes of secrecy, and a growing frustration and hostility among those still subject to the old authority and its ways.

[3] A. E. C. W. Spencer, in *The Clergy Review*, London, Dec. 1966, p. 918.

Censorship is institutionalized secrecy. It operates mainly in the Catholic church in terms of permissions and approvals for the writing of books and articles. The present canon law, in process of revision, forbids all Catholics to write or publish religious books or articles of any kind without the prior approval of a bishop, who normally exercises this function through a censor. The author has practically no rights—no discussion or appeal is provided for—if his book is rejected; he has no right to know even the name of the censor, and no clear right to demand a statement of his errors. There is a strong move among the canon lawyers for major legal reform in this area. In the meantime, many authors and publishers are circumventing or ignoring the whole matter. Many censors and bishops, also, are exercising the law liberally within its strictest limits of safeguarding essential Christian orthodoxy. However, this censorship remains in the church structure as a kind of communications denial, generating institutional thinking and role frustration.

My own experience of church censorship may illustrate the problem. My book *Priestly Celibacy and Maturity* was favorably censored and published in the United States in 1965. It was moderate in tone, urging further study of the problems I raised, and gently suggesting that celibacy might be for priests a matter of personal choice rather than of legal obligation. Of the reviews in some twenty Catholic journals which I have seen, none questioned the theological orthodoxy of the book, and almost all praised its thoughtful approach. However, when it came to the publishing of a French translation, the French censor demanded large-scale deletions, which had to be agreed to by the French publishing firm as they had already incurred large expenses with the book. I demanded to see the deletions, and I was amazed to find that they covered pages rather than paragraphs, and that the whole tone of the book had become more cautious than I could ever have been. The whole orientation of the book towards change and legal reform was censored out. I could only wonder whether I should try, at the last moment, to prevent the French publication entirely, or whether I should do nothing and get on with this present book, which I felt was much more important. A whole host of reasons urged me to make the latter decision.

Here, then, was a communication which was effectively blocked and distorted by censorship, an example of the way that narrow and safe thinking is institutionalized. It is not surprising that censorship has become one of the Church's own worst enemies. The list of the theologians whose books have been altered or forbidden, or who have been the subject of public admonitions and cautions during the past thirty or forty years, reads like a theologians' who's who. The loss to the church community of the working genius of Teilhard de Chardin during his life is quite incalculable. Here was an anthropologist-theologian whose life task was the bridging of the two thought systems in which he lived as a faithful and dedicated scholar. The Church, in effect, censored him out of existence during his lifetime; it is only through his works being published outside the church community after his death that we have had the tardy benefit of his challenging and controversial ideas.

Censorship undoubtedly has its effect in many unnoticed areas of Catholic life. One that concerns us most here is the consequently poor level of professional literature for priests and their meager reading habits in the areas relative to their role and its evolution. From many years of reading Catholic theological journals and books, I can suggest no blame for the clergy; the tragedy lies beyond their evident goodwill and patience. Censorship has taken from this kind of writing the qualities of newness, freshness and originality which make for interesting reading; one has a feeling, in reading the best of Catholic theologians, something like the sensation of driving a car with a governor on its accelerator. There is none of the mind-stretching quality, the eager reaching to the limit of thinking and beyond into tentative speculation, and the use of intellectual shock-tactics that liven and give originality to the writings of such Protestant theologians as Barth, Niebuhr, Cox or Robinson. Priests have pointed out to me that the general censorship laws of the Church forbid them to read these non-Catholic authors unless they are sure beforehand that they contain nothing contrary to the teaching of the Catholic church; however, I gather from many priests that they consider it essential to their modern role to be familiar with these writings, and that, in this period of legal reform, they consider these church laws outmoded and no longer binding.

This general suppression of communication at the most vital level within the Church, and all the accompanying attitudes of intellectual repressiveness and timidity which accompany it, has a kind of enervating effect on the total social organism. Deutsch explores the analogies of selfhood and consciousness in communication networks, and points out how the autonomy of a system, a social group or a person can be destroyed by depriving it of information about the state of its parts; he compares this situation to that of a man who is punch-drunk, or walking in his sleep. He goes on:

> A society or community that is to steer itself must, then, continue to receive a full flow of three kinds of information; first, information about the world outside; second, information about the past, with a wide range of recall and recombination; and third, information about itself and its own parts. Let any one of these three streams be long interrupted, such as by oppression or secrecy, and the society becomes an automaton, a walking corpse. It loses control over its own behavior, not only for some of its parts, but eventually also at its very top. Or let the monitoring of internal data be unimpaired, let consciousness exist, but inhibit its feedback into the behavior of the system—create a consciousness at once informed and powerless—and you have the pattern of a man who feels himself "possessed," who watches his own behavior in helpless surprise, unable to change it. On the level of a society, this is the experience of Cassandra watching her city rush to its doom.[4]

4 Marks, editor, *op. cit.*, p. 250.

A discussion in these terms about censorship in the Church is generally experienced as an attack on church authority; most priests, in discussing the present difficulties and confusions of their role, will come eventually to some expression of this anxiety, which they experience the more deeply because of their education and their life within the Church as it is. However, the view of the Church as a communications system does not destroy the concept of authority within the group; rather, it clearly demands some concept of authority analogous to the program and programmer for an electronic system.

There is no doubt in the minds of the priest, or of any Catholic, as to where this authority lies; the head of the Church, in whom all authority lies, is undoubtedly Christ. His authority, as presented in the New Testament, is always in relation to his mission as a messenger of God; it is the authenticity of the communication that is stressed. He forms a brotherhood of followers who listen to his message from the father in heaven, a message of human reconciliation in mutual love and care. The brotherhood must live by this message and themselves be the living message to all men.

The program and the programmer are clear enough; the difficulty of defining the roles and functions within this communicating group must be worked out in terms of the original programming. As the twelve apostles are seen in the New Testament as primary witnesses to the message and person of Christ and as the servants of the community, they remain a pattern for the present functioning of the group of bishops and that of the priests who share their task of witnessing and serving. But this witnessing and serving must clearly be in relation to the primary purpose of the group, that of communication of the father's message in Christ as a gift to all men, calling them to be united in love, care and mutual service.

As Deutsch points out in the above quotation, this functioning requires a full flow of three kinds of information. There must be information about the world outside, about the whole community of men for whom the Church exists as a communicating system, within which the Church lives and offers its message. There must be information about the past, about the original program which must be lived and presented authentically. In the person and word of Christ, therefore, is the "authority" of the system. By recall, also, the system is guided by ways of doing things, of solving problems, which have been recognized as authentic in its past experience, as it also rejects much other experience. In theological terms, this is the Church's tradition.

The third kind of information is about the system itself and its own parts and present functioning. By definition, the Church, as a human expression of a divine communication, is subject to all kinds of malfunctioning. It is essential, if change is to lead to improved functioning, that full information on the present state of the system flows freely and without suppression or distortion. This brings us to the practical problems of change within the church body, which we are discussing throughout this book in the focus of the changing role of the priest. Even here, the communications experts are helpful. The problem of communication systems are part of their ordinary expert concern; many of the systems they build are designed precisely to be self-steering, self-modifying, self-correcting in terms of their ultimate aim and of their constantly changing intermediate aims.

Deutsch deals with the problems of accelerated change in social groups, and points out that there may be various kinds of casualties among those unable to adapt positively to change. He suggests that the best solution lies in an increase of inner facilities for adjustment:

> To permit a high speed of learning and wide changes of behavior, without loss of inner structure and of an effective past, can perhaps best be accomplished by increasing the inner communications channels in variety, flexibility, and numbers. To insure continued self-determination, integrity and dignity are not enough. In the language of religion, pride may mean death where a change of heart

may mean survival. In less exalted terms, the best way to strengthen a communications system against the impact of large external changes may well consist in enriching its internal structure and its range of possible new configurations.[5]

The urgent task of the priest, in his present-day role, seems therefore to center round the problems of rapid change within the church group as it steers itself into new directions to meet its aims of communicating openly with the human community of today. The priest will serve his people best, in the strains and stresses they will experience through this change period, by making sure that existing channels of communications are open and that information is flowing freely. He should try to correct blockages and distorted perception of messages moving upward, downward and laterally within the group, from the church group to the human community, and from the community to the group. Priests themselves often enough will still be suffering from the various forms of communication blockage and denial that we have described in this chapter, and this will make a positive conception of their role doubly difficult. It seems to me that, whatever long-term discussion reveals about the shape of the priest role in the Church for the future, this task of the priest is immediately urgent and demanding.

If, as was suggested at the beginning of this chapter, we view liturgy and worship as a ritualized form of the whole communication function of the Church for the human community, the priest should find the task just outlined very close to the central concept of his priesthood. This task of helping to open up all the channels of communication, both within the Church and also outward and inward, is the required way of seeing to it that the message of God to men in the person, sayings and deeds of Christ becomes clearly available. The priest's concern, as mediator, is to make sure that men's response is heard and listened to, so that the Church can be readjusting its aims and directions to

5 *Ibid.,* p. 253.

meet their needs, their questions, their problems. This daily concern with the Word of God and with the affairs and hearts of men may well come to be expressed vividly in the reformed worship of the Church, in which this whole communication process could take on a particularly sharp reality.

Something of this view of the immediate priority of the priest's role is expressed by the Vatican Council in the Church's traditional language and thought forms:

> The people of God finds its unity first of all through the Word of the living God, which is quite properly sought from the lips of priests. Since no one can be saved who has not first believed, priests, as co-workers with their bishops, have as their primary duty the proclamation of the gospel of God to all. In this way they fulfil the Lord's command: "Go into the whole world and preach the gospel to every creature" (Mk. 16:15). Thus they establish and build up the people of God. For through the saving Word the spark of faith is struck in the hearts of unbelievers, and fed in the hearts of the faithful. By this faith the community of the faithful begins and grows. As the apostle says: "Faith depends on hearing, and hearing on the word of Christ" (Rom. 10:17). Toward all men, therefore, priests have the duty of sharing the gospel truth in which they themselves rejoice in the Lord.[6]

6 *The Documents of Vatican II*, Walter M. Abbott, editor (New York: Guild, America and Association Presses, 1966), pp. 538–539.

9: WHAT DO THEY SEE IN A PRIEST? / images and life style

How does the modern priest look to people? What is his image? What kind of life does he have? These questions are crucial in examining the evolving role of the Roman Catholic priest because role is a reciprocal affair. We form our working concept of who we are, and what we are for, in terms of what people see in us and expect of us. Fortunately, the process works the other way, too. People will tend to see in us what we see in ourselves; by our own rethinking of a role we can be reshaping the expectation that others experience when they meet us.

Here is how one modern Catholic sees the Church and its clergy. Michael Novak, in his book *Belief and Unbelief*, has a chapter on "Corruption and Community." Here he speaks of the general complacency and apathy of believers as a source of unbelief and draws a picture of the Church in America as a shell without a spirit. He tells of the activism of the clergy and their enthusiasm for building and money-raising, and quotes Marcel's description of American Catholicism as a sect jealous of its own interests, reputation and cohesiveness. Novak goes on:

— A high proportion of its bishops, the faithful complain, seem characteristically timid, prudent, cautious men whose great ideal is

154

not to step out of line, not to offend ecclesiastical proprieties, not to cause trouble, not to be tempted by a new idea. The clean-shaven monsignori who run the chancery, the school system, the seminaries, and the largest parishes, seem to be businessmen, golf-ers, connoisseurs of restaurants, well trained to the books of canon law, in love with the church as an institution, money raisers, ene-mies of "secularism," proud of the church as a bulwark against atheistic communism, good company for brother priests and for congenial parishioners, sometimes prayerful, and faithful eunuchs for the "kingdom of God." Is this the community of believers of which the Gospels speak?[1]

The reactions of readers to this last paragraph will be various, covering the whole range from "And that's not half the story!" to "This is utter nonsense—a biased and unfair picture"; and there will be all grades of judgment, suspended judgment, and lack of interest between the extremes. This serves to show us that we can speak of the image of the priest only in the way of an impressionist artist rather than in any scientific fashion. For those who prefer the language and method of social research, the books of Joseph Fichter and Marie Augusta Neal will be helpful; however, the present limitations of this kind of research are evident in their attempts, thorough as they are, to measure such a complex, varied and evolving social reality. It may be useful here to look at three simple areas of immediate experi-ence in the life of the priest, and to reflect on them in terms of the general image and expectations of his role. These three areas are the way in which he is addressed, the uniform he wears, and his general style and level of life.

HOW TO SPEAK TO A PRIEST

Paternalism has been a recurring theme in this book; in so many of the role situations we have looked at, this seemed to be the only way to sum up in a word what was going wrong. While I was writing this book, and as I realized that paternalism was

[1] Michael Novak, *Belief and Unbelief* (New York: Macmillan, 1965), pp. 183–184.

becoming a recurring theme, most people I met were calling me "Father." It made me wonder.

Many people during this time did not address me as Father, but called me David. I expect every man has a secret liking for the sound of his name that goes back to the love experience of early childhood. For me this old Jewish word, with its meaning of love and endearment, is the nicest word I hear; I have heard it so much from those who love me and from those who care for me as friends. While I was writing, then, and wondering about being "Father" and being paternalistic, I thought about the many people who called me David. They were my family; many friends from childhood days, some Catholics and others not; numbers of professional colleagues, priests, ministers, social workers, counselors, psychologists and the like; finally a few good friends, men and women, children and students, who somehow felt that my name honored me more than a title. I mention all this because there are some who might think that names and titles do not matter very much in the shaping of a man's role and relationships. For me this question moves right into the area that matters most in my life.

In our societies, when strangers meet they will use formal titles such as Mister, Professor, Doctor, for a time; but if their relationship begins to form into friendship, they will exchange Christian names. This, indeed, is the formalizing of a new relationship, and they will speak of being on a first-name basis with one another. This moment is very important to people, as we find when we try to hasten it and are met with an unresponsive coldness. People who use titles, in the services, in the academic, legal and medical professions, are generally regarded as unsociable, distant, and "standing on their dignity" if they insist on their titles beyond the moment of friendship.

I feel that priests lose a great deal by not following this custom. I feel that the constant use of a title brings an element of unnecessary formality and social distance into a priest's relation-

ship with people. The use of the title "Father" is particularly
unfortunate in that it gives a relationship an overtone which
represents a past social structure rejected by the modern priest.
It is unnecessarily difficult for him to reject the paternal submis-
sive relationship while the symbol of this relationship is constantly in his ear and in the other's voice; there is a very real
sense in which we are what we say, and we become what we
hear.

James Kavanaugh, a priest whose book on his outdated
Church is a cry of anguish for all that has gone wrong, devotes
two pages to this topic:

> I am never "Jim"; I am the patriarchal "Father," the man who
> sees but half of life and seldom hears the truth. People have been
> taught to fear me, to cater to me, to make few demands, to give me
> the benefit of the doubt. . . . I am "Father," the man who never
> has to know the misery that is man. No question puzzles me, no
> moral dilemma puts me off. The man who talks back to me is
> proud, the sinner who quarrels with me is unrepentant and obsti-
> nate. I am always right, always deserving of respect. My faults are
> excused, my ignorance overlooked, my immaturity condoned.[2]

If priests are to be real about a new view of their role, if they
are to be serious about seeing the Church no longer as a closed
society within society, a community within the community, they
must consider seriously the customs and styles which formalize
and ritualize their role. Where these forms and styles do not
correspond to the meaning and message they wish to convey in
their functioning, they should be changed. This is so particularly when the forms have no long tradition and consecrated
symbolic meaning. The title "Father" is of local use in the
Church, and of quite recent origin as an address for priests.
When we measure it against the authentic symbols and signs of
Christian tradition, we may conclude that it was never a very
suitable form; it was originally rejected as obscuring a much

2 James Kavanaugh, *A Modern Priest Looks at His Outdated Church* (New
York: Trident Press, 1967) , pp. 24–25.

more important symbol of fatherhood. Christ dealt directly with this problem; he attacked the religious functionaries of his time for taking the chief places at table and the first places in the synagogue, having their hands kissed and for being called "Rabbi." He went on to tell his followers:

> You are not to claim the title of Rabbi; you have but one Master, and you are all brethren alike. Nor are you to call any man on earth your Father; you have but one father, and he is in heaven. Nor are you to be called teachers; you have but one teacher, Christ. Among you, the greatest of all is to be the servant of all (Matthew 23:8–11).

The usual Catholic reaction to this saying of Christ is to reduce it to absurdity and to point out that surely Christ did not mean to prohibit altogether the use of the words master, father and teacher; he is using an exaggerated form of language to emphasize the ideal of equality and brotherhood in his group of followers. Which seems to me to miss the whole context and force of what he is saying; he criticized the Jewish religious leaders, not for any great sin or corruption, but for the small things that point to a deeper attitude because they are so symbolic and meaningful. He is pointing out that it is very difficult to be brothers and to have no social stratification, if titles of honor are being used.

What we have said of these titles applies all the more to the various honorifics which are used for the upper grades of the Catholic clergy: "Monsignor," "My Lord," "Your Excellency," "Your Eminence," "Your Beatitude," "Your Holiness." It might be argued that these are harmless relics of old social traditions which lend a little color and ritual to our lives, that they are on a par with calling an ambassador "Your Excellency," a judge "Your Honor," and a queen "Your Majesty." But the whole point of this chapter is that these titles, and that of "Father," are really much more important than harmless traditions. They determine a social distance, they distinguish a social group or caste, which should not exist at all. They were real in a period of church life which emphasized a distinction and a distance between clergy and laity which certainly serves no authentic purpose now, if it ever did. Finally, these titles of honor tend to be role-fixing and attitude-forming for both priest and people.

ON PRIESTS AND THEIR UNIFORM

In this book about priests and their changing role, it might appear trivial to be concerned about what a priest wears; the question of his uniform does not seem to be much more important than the current controversy in convents about the length of the nuns' skirts. If it seems thus, it may be a sign that this book has already done its damage. In writing, I have tried to keep reminding myself that role is a word and a priest is a person. Role is a convenient shorthand sign for a very complex interpersonal and group reality, but this reality never exists alone except on a page like this; in real life it can exist only in a person. In a book it is almost impossible to convey this reality as one can do in a seminar. In a seminar, persons are present, and no one but a fool would imagine that the role is more important than the person. And the real difficulty I see about priests wearing a uniform all the time is precisely that it seems to emphasize the role at the expense of the person. It is saying, loud and clear, "This is a priest," and it never says, "This is a person, a man, an individual, and his name is David."

We have discussed throughout this book the modern emphasis on being one's authentic self, on being a person, on being individual, on being different. The meeting of existentialism and personality psychology provides a scholarly and fruitful background to this popular emphasis. We saw that this is a necessary human reaction to the possible anonymity of large-scale urbanized life and to the impersonal economic shape of our societies. This is man's way of being real, of being fully human, in our kind of human community. So we pay increasing attention to the search for the authentic self, for the personal identity, for the meaning of the other, for the experience of community. We have seen that the Roman Catholic church has been responding to this human movement, however ponderously and ambiguously, and that the changing role of the priest is an evolving element in this response.

This kind of thinking and feeling makes us very aware of anything in our life or role that is impersonal, that emphasizes conformity rather than individuality. We take note of Jung's concept of the persona, the mask which the old classical actors used to wear in order to be someone else than their personal selves. We all have a tendency to hide our real selves, and we saw in our chapter on moral trends that our maturing as persons is, in part, a process of growing out of our need for pretence and unreality. When we view the constant wearing of a uniform in this light, we come to realize that it may no longer be functional for the priest as a person.

Josef Goldbrunner, a German psychologist, speaks of the dangers of masks and uniforms for those in the professions. He tells of the way a schoolteacher may carry his teaching role of authority and power home with him after school, so much so that he may identify himself as a role rather than a real person, and live behind a mask which eventually shapes and controls his life. He continues:

> All professions that have a wide scope of influence seem to embody that strong temptation for one to identify himself with the profession. For the most part such groups are associated with wearing uniforms: military personnel, clergy, academicians, and so forth. The white coat of the physician, for instance, greatly elevates the human position of its wearer—particularly since he is at all times connected with a situation of helping and healing. (Going beyond one's competence in vital questions is always a symptom of the mask.) In the context of pastoral care, the prime question is, of course, the mask of the pastor. The prestige of the pastoral office is enhanced by the fact that people tend to put the wearer of priestly

garb on a pedestal and expect him to respond to it with piety. Pride, or even more, inner unfulfillment, can fabricate his professional power into a stiff, brocaded vestment that he is not too eager to shed. Once he gets into it, he identifies himself with it. Inevitably his human behavior undergoes a process of change, until finally he can communicate with his flock only through a mask.[3]

Uniforms have performed many useful functions in man's history; originally, they served to distinguish friend from foe in hand-to-hand warfare. This quality of high visibility makes it still useful for some policemen to wear uniforms, and for doctors in hospitals. Uniforms have also been extensively used for denoting social class and status. It is not surprising, then, that uniforms have come to have a high symbolic and even religious value attached to them, as in some army regiments and in some convents. Uniforms have been widely used for disciplinary purposes, as in prisons; the old insistence in church law that priests must wear their uniform while on holiday seems to have some element of this.

It does not seem that a uniform offers much functional advantage to the priest in his modern role; the increasing number of priests who keep their uniforms for more formal and ecclesiastical occasions do not report any serious disadvantages. The matter should be judged in terms of the history, tradition and symbolism which has attached itself to the custom. In fact, the present clergy uniform is of quite recent origin, and there is no constant tradition in the Church about priests wearing uniforms, or as to what the style of the uniform should be. Several areas of the Church have, in recent times, made changes in the uniform for the clergy without notable disturbance or worry. It seems that there is little in favor of uniforms for priests to outweigh the positive advantage of abolishing them or keeping them for formal occasions only. Once again, if we question priests' uniforms in the light of the original symbols and meanings of

[3] Josef Goldbrunner, *Realization* (Notre Dame, Indiana: University of Notre Dame Press, 1966) , pp. 68–69.

Christian discipleship, we find that this custom does not contribute to the authenticity of the role of the priest.

John McKenzie, from his viewpoint of scriptural scholarship, is highly critical of all elements which seem to dignify authority and status in the church community. He comments:

> One can understand why our predecessors thought that spiritual authority should be vested with an external splendor which symbolized the dignity of authority. We can understand it, even if we think they were wrong in adopting the trappings of secular princes. One should also be able to understand the impatience of modern people with these antiquated trappings. Modern people live in a world where the state uniform of the head of the most powerful nation in the world is a business suit—and it is in the same garb that other heads of state appear. Even in the armed services, which are second only to the ecclesiastical profession in the love of pageantry, the general wears little to distinguish him from the private soldier in combat; the magnificent dress uniforms of generals and admirals are becoming more and more rare, and they are scarcely worn except at formal balls and diplomatic receptions. When the secular state can dispense with the symbolic apparatus of royalty and nobility, it seems that the ecclesiastical polity, which has in its foundation documents a warning against such apparatus, could even more quickly dispense with it. Originally devised to increase prestige, ecclesiastical pomp is now helping to destroy that which it was intended to support.[4]

THE PRIEST'S STYLE OF LIFE

We have stressed that, in giving some positive direction to the changes taking place in his role, the Catholic priest should keep in mind three factors: the contribution which any element under discussion makes towards the present and overall goals of the church brotherhood; the symbolic and traditional meanings associated with the matter under discussion; and what might be judged of it in terms of original role authenticity as seen in the New Testament.

[4] John L. McKenzie, *Authority in the Church* (New York: Sheed and Ward, 1966), p. 106.

A major task for the priesthood is to consider, in the light of these three factors, the whole life style of the clergy in our society. This will be a continuing task as conditions of life within the Church, and in the wider community, are developing. The steps being taken in the Church to establish a married clergy, many of whom will be engaged in other occupations, is a major change that will have some effect on the life of all the clergy, married and celibate, full-time and part-time. This change alone may well lead to a much more specialized role for the priest; this in turn will create an increased demand for more flexible relationships of an interprofessional type. Writing of the pressures of change in clergy-lay relationships, Sister Marie Augusta Neal discusses the effect of more specialized function:

> in the process of structural differentiation which has been going on in western society since the beginning of the Christian era, the family is no longer a universally functionally effective model. The economy, the policy, and other social systems have goals which necessitate more peer-like relations in the interdependencies that have developed with the specialization of function. These systems also require greater resiliency in moving from the leader to the follower role than is possible in a system that particularizes the leader role in a stable family model. Within the church, however, the family model characteristic of the peasant-elite society of the middle ages persisted as the valued role relation between clergy and laity. This persistence generated problems of dependency and rebellion that characterize certain parish experiences today and give rise to pressures to redefine legitimate clergy-laity relations by the church.[5]

Whatever the future may hold in this direction, there are many elements for examination in the present life style of the priest. The strong criticisms of clergy life voiced by many lay people and a few of the clergy in recent years, of which the quotation from Michael Novak on page 155 gives an example, point the direction for some of this examination. It is easy enough for any intelligent Catholic to question whether the present style of

[5] Marie Augusta Neal, *Values and Interests in Social Change* (Englewood Cliffs, N.J.: Prentice-Hall, 1965), p. 29.

life of the Pope, living as he does in a renaissance palace with a wealth of pomp and ceremonial, is really functional for the Church of our day; to question also whether the traditional and symbolic elements in his life style are worth preserving; and to examine the papal life style in the light of the demands of the New Testament for community leadership in terms of equality, brotherhood and service. A similar examination of the life style of bishops and priests is called for if the process of role renewal is to develop smoothly. The style of living chosen by the clergy is a vital type of communication; if elements of inconsistency and contradiction are allowed to remain, the whole communication role of the priest becomes confused and uncertain, and is experienced by lay people as ambiguous.

The examination of the images and style of the clergy in relation to their role, if thoroughly done, would merit a much larger book than this one. A good deal of study and research, covering many other key areas than the three mentioned in this chapter, would be a necessary preliminary. This kind of study, and the discussion of practical issues which would follow, might well be a useful project to be promoted by some of the professional groups of priests, priests' senates and pastoral councils.

10:FROM CELIBATE TO MARRIED / *a discussion that would not die*

One of the factors affecting the role of the Catholic priest has been the gradual change of church law and custom on the celibate state of the clergy. It has been evident for some years that the Church is moving away from the situation whereby all of its clergy in the West would be bound by church law to remain unmarried. This change of law has been basically a community response to the many movements of thought and opinion which have been described in this book from the viewpoints of psychology, sociology, philosophy and ethics. In terms of the evolving self-image of man, his search for identity and maturity, and the importance given in this search to interpersonal relationships and sexual fulfillment, the legal aspects of the priest's form of self commitment have inevitably come to take second place to the aspect of personal choice and individual dedication. A second major influence in the background of this change has been the movement towards corporate union between the various Christian churches; the Roman Catholic church, while not wishing to lose its distinctive message on dedicated celibacy, must move to a more flexible position in view of the negotiations for a reunion which seems, sociologically speaking, quite inevitable.

It is significant that the first signs of change in the Catholic law of celibacy for the Western clergy came when exceptions began to be made for married ministers of other churches who wished to become Catholics and to continue their ministry. This was taken by many observers of the time as an indicator of a new development, which has since, in fact, been going ahead. The general ambiguity, the secrecy and the apparent lack of overall planning in this development is, for the Catholic church, normal enough; unfortunately it has the result, as in other areas, of heightening the sense of confusion among priests.

A second sign of change became evident, without any announcement or interpretation to priests, when they found out, here and there, that some of their colleagues had resigned from the ministry and had been married in secret with the Church's full blessing. This new flexibility, so innocuous by normal standards, was a radical change from the severity of former days when priests, to become married, had to leave the Church altogether and incur the severest condemnation and excommunication. This new procedure has been kept so secret that many priests of my acquaintance who wished to make use of it had the greatest difficulty in finding anyone who could help them. Here is a kind of communication denial, which, if it were designed to increase anxiety and confusion, could only be marvelled at. Without hope of help from this cumbersome, secretive and slow working administrative machinery, comparatively large numbers of priests have continued to leave their ministry and marry without the blessing of the Church.

The third and most decisive step so far toward a married clergy for the Church was decided on at the Vatican Council; the bishops provided for the restoration of the order of deacons as an active ministry in the Church. They decided that this ministry would be open to "men of more mature age, even those living in the married state." Regulations announced in June, 1967, fixed the mature age at thirty-five years. Deacons were an important part of the Church's clergy in former times; they carried out all the present functions of the priest except those of hearing confessions and being the celebrant of the Mass. The new regulations allow for married deacons to carry on work in other occupations. It is impossible to estimate what the general effect of this restoration may be; it is clear that the present image of the Catholic clergy as a group of full-time professionals who must be unmarried will be substantially changed.

Along with the regulations on the choice, training and work of married deacons for the Church wherever bishops decided on this change, Pope Paul VI issued an encyclical letter on the law of celibacy for priests in the Western areas of the Church. This letter stressed that the changes being introduced should not be taken as a prelude to the general abolition of the law of celibacy for priests. The Pope reviewed many arguments in favor of keeping celibacy as a matter of personal option for priests rather than of law, and went on to a long theological discussion of the fittingness of keeping the present law in force. Conceding that celibacy is not demanded by the nature of the Christian priesthood, and giving full praise to the married priests in the Eastern areas of the Church, he developed the theological and historical background of the Western tradition of priestly celibacy.

This positive statement does not obscure the fact of substantial modification of the traditional law. The Church is clearly providing for a married clergy in the restoration of the order of deacon. The Pope also makes quite official the exceptions that are being made for married ministers of other churches who wish to join the Catholic communion and to carry on their ministry. And, in a lengthy part of his letter, he describes openly the dispensations from the law which are being granted to those priests who wish to give up their ministry and be married within the Church. While this section of the letter is ambiguously written and leaves studiously unclear the conditions and process of gaining these dispensations from the celibacy law, the unveiling to this extent of the cloak of secrecy is itself a major change in Roman procedure. In spite of the Pope's eulogies of the present law, these changes give every indication that they are part of a gradual process of development within the Catholic community. It seems likely, when these trends are seen as part of the overall picture of a changing profession, that the process will move fairly rapidly to a point where celibacy will remain as a specially recommended type of personal commitment for priests, depending on mature personal decision rather than on church law.

In the meantime, in spite of admonitions that this delicate matter should be left to the Pope and bishops to decide, a widespread public debate has been going on among priests and lay people about the value and wisdom of having a celibate clergy. My own book on the celibacy and maturity of the priest was written at a time when almost nothing had appeared in English on this topic; by the time it was published, a few books had been translated from other languages into English, and articles were appearing frequently in learned journals, newsmagazines and religious periodicals. In particular, the *National Catholic Reporter,* of Kansas City, Missouri, featured a long series of articles and letters, many from distinguished psychologists and theologians, during 1966. The same paper helped promote a survey on this and related topics by Joseph Fichter, a Jesuit sociologist working at Harvard.

From a questionnaire mailed to a sampling of diocesan priests, excluding pastors, Fichter gained a fifty-one percent response—over 3,000 replies. To a question, "In general, would you be in favor of the diocesan priest's freedom of choice to marry?" forty-seven percent replied with a clear approval, and another fifteen percent gave a qualified approval, some favoring marriage before ordination only, others favoring marriage after ordination. Asked if they themselves would marry if allowed, thirty-one percent gave some positive answer, five percent saying "unquestionably would," nine percent "very likely," and seventeen percent "probably would." Fichter, in an interview, said

that he was not surprised by the strong majority favoring freedom on the choice of celibacy or marriage. Pointing out that many more favored freedom than expressed a wish to marry, he said that most priests "are in favor of it but don't want to do it themselves. They have patterned themselves as bachelors, and I have an idea they're not too anxious to break the pattern, but they're not against the idea for others." On another response, he said that he was somewhat surprised—"in a rather negative way"—by the number who thought that there should be some kind of "out," some way of resigning honorably from the priesthood.[1]

Sixty-four percent of the respondents had endorsed the idea of permitting resignations from the priesthood as from other professions.

Taking fully into account the limitations of this kind of survey, we are left with a strong expression of clergy opinion. A large proportion of the American clergy favor the removal of celibacy from the field of church law to that of personal commitment and choice. A substantial number of them would definitely like to get married if they were allowed to by church law, and there is strong belief in the idea of a change of vocation being a matter of personal decision. Other surveys of this type have been carried out recently, and with varying methods and results they confirm these general conclusions.

Like Fichter, I was not surprised at the survey results. Following the publication of my book on this subject, I lectured and conducted seminars for priests and seminarians widely throughout the United States in 1966. I concluded that a large proportion of priests, especially in the younger age groups, and even more of the seminarians, were in favor of changing the law. There was a general feeling that the positive values of celibacy as a form of Christian commitment would be better served by making it a matter of personal choice.

[1] Reported in *The National Catholic Reporter*, Kansas City, Missouri, December 14, 1966.

The strong connection between personal identity and the image of one's role in society was stressed in all these discussions. Celibacy was seen as a determinant of identity and role, as were other socially approved forms of sexual commitment. Being a dedicated celibate is part of the answer to the two questions, "Who am I?" and "What do I do?" For this reason, it was felt that the continuing decision about celibacy should not be experienced as coming from the outside in a legal obligation, but from within the person. Under the present church law, the original choice of a celibate state before ordination to the priesthood was certainly a matter of decision for the seminarian; however, this choice was experienced by many as impersonal and unfree because of the clear condition: if the seminarian does not choose celibacy, he must give up the idea of being a priest. The position on celibacy which emphasized free decision rather than law was the one I had taken in my book; it seemed to be the position a large body of the clergy and seminarians were taking, or were at least tentatively considering.

However, in the meantime others were asking more searching questions, doubting the positive value of dedicated celibacy from the psychological and theological viewpoints. Some psychologists were suggesting in discussion that the positive values of growth and fulfillment involved in the sexual relationship were such that a deliberate and final rejection of this relationship seemed highly suspect. While it was possible to conceptualize a decision for permanent celibacy in terms of a higher motivational pattern of religious or humanist values, in practice this would usually be at the expense of normal human maturity and fulfillment, particularly in middle life. Those who proposed this opinion would allow for a choice of permanent celibacy only in cases of the charismatic leader, the "man with a mission," who operated in terms of unusually intense patterns of work and motivation. They suggested that it was wrong to institutionalize as a law for a large group something that was a highly unusual form of human adjustment. One psychologist, discussing the use made by church authorities of the example of Christ as a model for the clergy, reminded me of one of Jung's remarks which I had quoted in my book on celibacy:

> Are we to understand the "imitation of Christ" in the sense that we should copy his life . . . or in the deeper sense that we are to live our own proper lives as truly as he lived his in all its implications? It is no easy matter to live a life that is modelled on Christ's, but it is unspeakably harder to live one's own life as truly as Christ lived his.[2]

A storm of controversy rose in 1966 when Dan Sullivan presented a psychologist's view of several current Catholic viewpoints on sexual matters; he spoke of a residual attitude of biologism which underlay much current thinking on marriage, contraception and celibacy. He stated:

> For anyone choosing freely to permanently and systematically "give up" sexual love and union, while simultaneously supporting the natural-law tradition that forbids deliberate self-mutilation, must logically, a priori, deny that sexual desire represents an integrally personal passion, one springing essentially from the whole person, and must deny that sexual union is a unique pathway to self-discovery, self-disclosure and self-fulfilment. The sexual ascetic must put a brake, at some decisive point, to every personalist movement occurring in sexual debates—this at the price of believing that he has not made his own self defective.[3]

On the theological side, a drawn-out discussion considered the role of the priest in general, and celibacy as a mode of Christian life. Catholic theologians, meeting other Christian ministers in depth discussions of theology and Christian ministry, often found that these ministers, at the existential level, experienced wife and family as an enrichment of Christian ministry rather than as an obstacle. A scholarly article by Rosemary Ruether reviewed the relationship of celibacy and radical discipleship in

---

[2] Carl Jung, *Modern Man in Search of a Soul* (New York: Harcourt, Brace & World, 1933) , p. 273.
[3] Dan Sullivan, in *The National Catholic Reporter*, June 29, 1966, p. 6.

the history of the Church. It described how, after the original enthusiasm of the early eschatological fellowship of Christians passed, radical discipleship came to be a separate mode of life within the Church; it expressed itself in terms of abstinence from sexual intercourse, from food, and from worldly involvement. After viewing the effects of the Reformation and of contemporary theologies of secularity and of crisis, the article locates the present crisis of the celibate ethic within this perspective:

> The crisis exists because we no longer believe that celibacy has any absolute relationship to radical discipleship. Thus its whole rationale is undermined at the roots. At the same time there is emerging a new ethic of radical discipleship which seems much more satisfactorily to relate the christological mode of being with finite historical existence. In this ethic, celibacy in the sense of "virginity" has no essential place. This does not mean, however, that the single life has no function at all in that new ethic . . . such a new appropriation of celibacy within the framework of a new eschatological ethic would necessarily remain personal and tenative. It has a pragmatic rather than a theological relationship to the "new creation" and could not be made subject to permanent vows. Having no absolute function in the relationship between secular and christological existence, it is unavailable for institutionalization.[4]

The role question of the Catholic clergy needs to be seen, then, within this larger question of his celibate or married role as a human person; this is a basic human determinant which is central to a man's identity and orientation. The question raised by Sullivan, in the article quoted above, seems to be whether a man can, normally speaking, deliberately set aside in a permanent commitment the positive values of marriage. It is suggested that this is to deny oneself an element of growth and fulfillment which is, normally speaking, essential. While many single people make various adjustments to an unmarried state which may be, in some cases, permanent, this kind of adjustment cannot be

4 Rosemary Ruether, in *The Christian Century*, October 19, 1966, p. 1270.

elevated into a distinct personal mystique. To do so seems to be a kind of immaturity response, widespread certainly, but hardly suitable to be made a matter of law for a large group.

Those who argue along these lines would find some support from the theological viewpoint of Rosemary Ruether; they would agree with her suggestion that celibacy may have, in various situations of church ministry, a pragmatic value of a high order. They would agree, too, that the highly gifted charismatic individual and the prophetic witness are types of highly motivated persons of unusual gifts. For these celibacy may seem to be an unescapable condition of their mission and vocation. At the same time, this unusual combination of gift and mission should not be made into a norm, much less a law, for others. In this argument, Christ would be seen as such a prophetic and charismatic personality, and it would be noted that, while he remained unmarried, he did not impose celibacy on his followers, nor did they for their successors in the early Church.

It seems, then, that this subject should continue to be examined in terms of the role and functioning of the priest, so that the development of law, custom and thinking which we have sketched may proceed on a more firm base of theory and research. As with other aspects of the priest's role, this continuing examination should be oriented to the changing function of the priest; it may well be found that celibacy is more functional in some situations, and marriage is more functional in others. In this discussion, the experience of the other Christian churches will be relevant, as will the experience of those areas within the Catholic communion which have both a married and a celibate clergy. The matter should be examined, also, in terms of its historical and symbolic value within the Catholic group and in this group's working relationship with the human community. Finally, the question should be reexamined in terms of role authenticity, as has been suggested with other topics for discussion; some kind of relationship of priesthood and celibacy is often vaguely suggested in church documents, and this relationship might be examined and properly qualified.

This aspect of the role of the priest is, as we have seen, undergoing rapid modification. There is, among priests, a sense of some crisis on this issue precisely because their sexual commitment affects so deeply their identity as persons and their role as professionals in our society. This sense of crisis has been heightened by a lack of communication on the issues involved in the change which is under way; the change so far has been dealt with in legalistic terms and without open discussion and consultation among priests. Here, again, is a communications denial which can have only unsatisfactory consequences; priests are widely feeling that they are being treated as servants who are not trusted to reason for themselves on this highly personal issue.

It has been my experience, in lectures and seminars, that a good deal of hostility has been generated on this topic among priests and seminarians; this hostility centers around the experience of having their central life commitment discussed at higher levels without their being involved in any consultation. This non-communication tends to undermine the group confidence of priests and their satisfaction in carrying out a valued role. This role demands so much in terms of life meaning and personal commitment that a sense of not being trusted to discuss one's own life patterns inevitably leads to frustration and inefficiency.

11: ON THE DISAPPEARING CLERGY / and finding a new role

This book has a loose stance, like a fencer who keeps mobile to face a constantly moving opponent. The reality it considers is a social reality of process, of change, of evolution. It views this mobile, evolving reality in terms of persons and their growth and identity searching; it looks at the roles and functions which are the ongoing expression of their mutuality with others; it relates them to groups and communities which are themselves searching and evolving. It sees these interacting processes in the light of experience, of presence, of communication, of power, and of energies of growth and change. It considers its social reality existentially rather than essentially, in terms of relations rather than of categories.

This general viewpoint seems to me to be the one which throws the clearest light on the present situation of the Roman Catholic priest and on his changing role in the Church and in the community. It is a viewpoint which is assumed by much of the psychology and sociology of our time. We have been able, then, to use the insights, theories and, to some extent, the research work of these disciplines to illumine the priest's issues and problems. Many priests, however, have pointed out to me that this viewpoint is itself a metaphysical assumption which, they feel, may be inadequate for a discussion of the religious values central to the life and orientation of the priest. They have emphasized that the priest is committed to an unchanging core of revealed truth which gives a stable center to his function in the Church; there are, therefore, certain essential factors in the work of a priest which are not subject to the processes of social change. While these priests would admit that sociology and psychology can offer assistance to a consideration of the role of the priest, they feel that this is secondary to the primary importance of the unchanging religious reality of priesthood. They will easily admit that the elements of change and development are much more extensive than was previously thought, but they would add that there is a limit to change, that there are basic religious essentials which can never change.

It would be tempting to take up the challenge of this thinking, to explore fully the notion of priesthood, with its associated roles of prophet and king, in the light of the dynamic of the Judaic and Christian tradition and historical development. But this would be to begin another book rather than to end this one. It is right, however, to comment that no sociologist would deny the reality and importance of the continuity of the role of the priest, nor the elements of authenticity which seem to be central to its system of meanings and expectations. What he might well doubt is that any clear distinctions and divisions can be made or conceptualized between what is essential and what is historically conditioned, between the unchangeable and the changeable. The processes of life, of maturation, of vital change, insofar as we can understand them at present, do not seem to leave much room for this kind of distinction; our growing understanding does not seem to be helped by this kind of divided thinking. In practice, I have taken the position that priesthood is seen more clearly in terms of role and role expectation, as a relational concept marked by an evolving mutuality and by the continuity of being lived in an historic community structure. I feel that the other position which I have described tends to objectify an unchanging essence, to reify non-change. This seems to make it difficult to conceive of the accidental features of change and historical conditioning in terms of true growth and vital process; it seems to give priority to the objective rather than the relational.

I have given some attention to this discussion for a further reason which touches directly on the present role of the priest as an agent of change within the church group. He is confronted, both in his own mind and in his interpretation of the Church of today to others, by the question, "How far can change go in the Church?" It is in terms of our metaphysical discussion above that he may choose either to answer: "The change in the Church will not affect anything essential, any central truths of faith or morals, but only the nonessentials," or, on the other hand, "The Church is growing, like ourselves or like a family, and everything that grows must accept change and newness. Just as your family has changed over the past ten years, but has still remained the same family, so the Church is changing rapidly while still remaining the same Church."

Eugene Fontinell, in an essay called "Reflections on Faith and Metaphysics," points out that while many changes have taken place in the Roman Catholic church in recent years, there is considerable divergence about the implications of change. He feels that many conservative Catholics have a more realistic view of what the changes may involve than many of their liberal opponents. The liberal, says Fontinell,

> argues that change can take place in the accidentals without touching the essentials, that it is possible to maintain absolutely immutable doctrines side by side with mutable expressions and understanding of those doctrines. This latter position, which characterizes most liberal American Catholic thinkers (and indeed most Catholics throughout the world), will, I suggest, run more and more into

difficulty. It may be that theirs is the best possible interpretation of Catholicism . . . if this is so, then in all honesty we should admit that Catholics cannot really integrate the results of the great revolutions in thought which have occurred over the last four hundred years, and in particular those of the last hundred years. My conviction, however, is this: the conservatives have more fully grasped the nature of change. We have set out on waters more treacherous than most liberals can admit. Change will in the future affect "immutable" truth.[1]

Fontinell goes on to describe the challenge of the processive view of reality and its place in contemporary metaphysics, and continues:

For the contemporary man it is reality and not simply an aspect or dimension of reality which is in process. In place of a world of substantial things extrinsically related he offers a world of "fields" or constellations of focused relations. In the contemporary world, process and relation rather than structure and substance are the controlling categories.[2]

It is within this view of reality in process that we have seen the changing role of the Catholic priest; he is trying to carry out a priestly function within a changing society, mediating a depth of meaning to men whose view of reality he may not share. This book began with a consideration of the challenge which the changing role of the priest presents to him in terms of his own identity as a person; he shares the uneasy feeling of many of the guardians of the traditions of our society that nothing now is sure and permanent, nothing too sacred to undergo change. We saw the Roman Catholic church coming to meet this challenge of change with an outdated system of structures and communications; we considered the feeling of many priests that the Church was dealing with yesterday's problems in the language of the day before. This experience could only be described as crisis in the priesthood, seen very differently by different priests, and by various of the authority figures in the Church, but felt

1 Eugene Fontinell, in Cross Currents, Winter, 1966, pp. 19–20.
2 Loc. cit.

by all as a sense that things were going wrong in some fairly urgent way, that decisions had to be made quickly, that whatever decision was made seemed to lead only to further difficulty and confusion.

In succeeding chapters, this book examined the priest's changing role and the change of status which has resulted. We saw the changing function and position of the priest in areas of family guidance and marriage counseling; we looked at his expertise in theology, in church affairs, and in parish administration. We saw something about the meaning of confusion in the life of the priest, and of the importance of getting issues and conflicts out into open discussion. We looked at social change as a challenge to the freedom of a priest, as he either withdraws into a narrow concern with the affairs of his ecclesiastical subculture, or tries to react with initiative in shaping a new position and role for himself. We saw how some of the personal attitudes of submissiveness and conformity operate against the use of initiative and free adaptation of his role, and how the conditions of creativity can operate in a priest or in a group of priests.

We discussed the security of the priest in his role as guardian of traditional morality, and the hesitancy with which he approaches the new emphasis on personal decision, responsible judgment and primacy of conscience as ideals of Christian living. We saw some implications of this in areas of church life, particularly in the evolving concept of sin and personal guilt. We looked at its effect on the priest's role as moral guide to adults and to children, and on the moral ideal of human maturity to which he aims to lead them. We concluded that the priest is left in a good deal of honest doubt as to where he stands, a doubt compounded by emotional confusion and anxiety about his role.

In several chapters the focus of attention was on the authority role of the priest and the way it is evolving in response to the conditions of modern life and to changing ideals within the church brotherhood; we looked at the ambiguity of this development as it coexists with the strong emphasis on authority within the Church and on the priest as the local agent of church authority. We looked at the double bind situation in this and several other areas of the priest's role, stressing the anxiety that comes from a crisis point in which any possible decision seems to be wrong and hurtful. Whether the priest chooses the traditional authoritarian way of interpreting his role, the ambivalence of liberal paternalism, one of the radical ways of innovation, or, as often happens, a mixture of all three, his confusion of identity and role may well be serious. Around the halfway point of the book we found ourselves beginning to explore the positive elements at work in the Church towards a reformulation of the priest's role. We looked at Christ's attitude to authority and the community shape which the apostles gave to his ideal of equality and brotherhood; we saw the development of authority structure in the Church's history and the way in which social class and social distance came to mark off the authority figures in the Church. The central point of role crisis here is in the contrast between the priest's functioning as agent of a complex, impersonal, authoritarian system, and his modern concern with the New Testament ideals of brotherhood, equality and mutual, personal care.

We passed on to look at the new social forms which a concern for freedom, initiative and shared responsibility were generating in the Church, at the effect of the theory and practice of sociology and psychology on emerging church structures, and on the new working models which priests are finding as they modify their role. Various radical viewpoints within the Church were examined, and their effect on the life and functioning of priests was assessed.

The book went on to look at the Church as a communications system and at the priest as the central point of a communications net; some consideration was given to the operation of paternalism, secrecy and censorship in the modern Church. Here we saw the modern role of the priest in terms of a clear demand that he work actively to ensure the free flow of information within the Church, upward, downward and laterally.

Towards the end of the book, we looked at some practical matters of image and life style of the priest in relation to new conceptions of his role, stressing the importance of the social forms which ritualize a role and convey its meaning. We considered the criteria of group functioning, symbolic meaning and role authenticity on which discussion of such matters as forms of address, uniforms and celibacy should be based. The importance of open communication on these subjects, both within the church group and without, was emphasized.

Looking back through this book, I feel that there is a good deal of projection into the future implicit in many of my observations and insights. To fill out this projection, it may be useful to discuss a few observations of a type which will, I think, occupy the increasing attention of priests in the years to come. Terence Eagleton, the young Cambridge scholar whose provocative ideas have already been quoted, feels concern that some of the emerging images of the priest of the future suggest a freezing of the kind of role development we are hoping for:

> The kind of image which is commonly offered to replace the outdated authoritarian models is that of the priest as a man coordinating and guiding the social and spiritual activity of a dynamic parish community, a man genuinely committed to the creation of community and responsibility among Christians, a focal point of social and moral welfare, which he can foster with the aid of sociological and psychological training, industrial experience, and so on. I think this image may have to be decisively rejected. . . .[3]

I agree with this opinion quite strongly. At the same time I would point out that, in the immediate situation of parish life as it is, the image which Eagleton rejects describes the kind of

[3] Terence Eagleton, *The New Left Church* (Baltimore: Helicon, 1966), p. 105.

priest who is doing what is immediately urgent; he is dealing with the backlog of remedial community work. Much preparation may have to be done before many of the positive ideals of which people like Eagleton speak so convincingly can be seen in true perspective. Channels of communication urgently need to be opened, and a sense of communal responsibility may need to be created almost from nothing. Some focal point of concern that will give the motivation to be a dynamic and caring group of Christians will have to be made present. In many cases, in the beginning, this new energy must come largely from the local priest, if it is to come at all. As a new growth comes, there will be new functioning, and a new variety of roles in which the priest may have to search keenly for his proper place.

Eagleton, and many others, feel that the one essential place of the priest is that of president of the Church in its liturgy, of witnessing to the word of God where Christians are assembled together for worship. As to what this will involve, in terms of time and personal concern, in terms of life role and professional training, we can only speculate. If the ideal at which to aim is a fully responsible group of Christians acting as a witnessing body, a communications group, for men around them in all stages of partial commitment and non-commitment, a group which is self-actualizing, self-teaching and self-caring, the life and image of the priest would certainly be very different from what it is today.

This thinking suggests a view of the Church in terms of fully responsible group life among Christians, and a task of open witnessing to men. This group offers itself as a communication for the human community at the level of life meaning, of human aims, of the shaping of human community in mutuality, love and new growth. If this picture comes to be accepted as the meaning of the Christian Church, it may well imply the disappearance of the clergy as a profession. It may well be that the active Christian groups of the future might experience the presence of a full-time professional priest as a denial of what their Christian commitment means to them. The full-time priest may be seen only as an outdated blockage in a communicating system of "real-life-meaning-fulfilment-destiny" lived out in the urgent affairs of the human community. In this picture, the only Christians who would be professionals would be a few scholars and specialists around the universities—if, that is, the full-time university teacher has any longer life expectation than the professional priest.

This may appear to some to be a far out forecast of a distant future. It seems to me that many of the dynamic trends we have looked at are pointing in this direction. For many years much attention was directed to French experiments involving priests working in factories; it seems that, with little attention, an increasing proportion of priests in the other Western countries have been spending most of their working time at tasks that bear only a small relation to the traditional pastoral concerns of the Church. We have seen, too, that the more varied skills and competencies of the young priests at present in training will open to them many areas of community work which will appear to them much more absorbing and important than the suburban parish. The regulations covering the ministry of deacons makes clear provision for a part-time clergy, and it seems inevitable that increased responsibility in the Christian ministry of lay people will lead to a devaluing of the services of a professional clergy.

The Roman Catholic church has a huge staff of full-time workers, men and women, clerical and lay. A rough estimate gives a rate of one full-time worker to about three hundred lay people. In the prosperous areas of the West, full-time workers are relatively more numerous; in New Zealand, the rate is one full-time worker to each one hundred Catholics. It would be surprising if the trends of church renewal did not produce a major change in this rate. Already the signs of a lower intake into seminaries and convents have produced much discussion of a "vocations crisis"; it may well be that this is a beginning of a process of de-institutionalizing of the church structure and its personnel.

This process is openly welcomed in a recent essay by Monsignor Ivan Illich on "The Vanishing Clergyman." He describes the growth of bureaucratic machinery in the Church as an organization explosion which is self-defeating, and "serves to make an already over-staffed church more priest-ridden, thereby debilitating the church's mission in today's world." He discusses the large numbers of resignations from the clergy and the defensive fashion in which this disturbance is rationalized:

> some explain clerical "defections" as the elimination of undesirable elements. Others blame the various contemporary mystiques of the world. The institution instinctively attempts to explain this loss and the concomitant vocation "crisis" in terms flattering to itself. Then, too, one needs strong justification for the enthusiastic and emotional drives for more "vocations." Few wish to admit that the collapse of an overextended and disproportionate clerical framework is a clear sign of its irrelevance.

Illich considers the various schemes on the retraining of the professional clergy for new skills within the Church; he suggests that priests should rather seek training in order to move right out into the secular world, renouncing the privileges and securities of the clerical group. In order to promote more quickly this disestablishment of the Church from within, Illich calls for priests who will

> leave the clergy in order to pioneer the church of the future . . . priests who, faithfully dedicated to and loving the church, risk misunderstanding and suspension. For priests, full of hope, capable of such actions without becoming hard and embittered. For extraordinary priests, willing to live today the ordinary life of tomorrow's priest.[4]

4 Ivan Illich, "The Vanishing Clergyman," in The Critic, June–July, 1967, pp. 18–27.

I find myself agreeing with such writers as Illich and Eagleton in their assessment of present trends and future tendencies for the life of priests. To me, these considerations seem vastly more important and indicative of the future than many current concerns of the clergy for a more thorough professionalization of their life and status. These concerns, sketched lightly in the Vatican Council's document on the priest, and made into a practical program by the Association of Chicago Priests and by other groups, are certainly valid enough as present aims. Many groups of priests, and priests' senates, have taken up these concerns for the training of priests in modern community work, for a rational system of payment for priests, a decent retirement scheme, a modern personnel and appointment policy, the treating of priests as responsible, adult, professional men of their time, and so on. This is all to the good for the present. It would, however, be rash to suppose that these overdue reforms will solve the problems that we have been discussing; these problems are much more deep-seated than is commonly considered in the many discussions of professional reform which I have heard in such groups of priests. Both the short-term and long-term tendencies of major change in the life of priests may make these professional reforms irrelevant at an early date.

I feel that this view of mine is well-based on what can be seen at the moment in terms of emerging role change, but it is still necessary to deal quickly and effectively with a great number of immediate concerns of the type discussed in the above paragraph. There is, too, a burden on the professional priest of today to accept his life as it is for the moment, as well as to plan his future. As new growth takes root, there will be new functioning of group life, and a new variety of roles appearing in which the priest may have to search keenly for his proper place at that moment. This will demand from the priest, while he is meditating on the larger issues raised in this chapter, a great flexibility and tolerance of change if he is to promote a new kind of active Christian grouping. The priest of today must certainly live and find his present meaning in the real Church of today; he must find his beginning point in present reality. It is from the Christians of today and from the structures of today that new attitudes and new forms must grow.

It would be tempting to begin here a chapter of the theology of the priesthood, to try to point a way to synthesize what I have written with traditional theological concepts. However, I have set out, from the beginning, to write from the viewpoints of sociology and psychology and in the style of personal insight. I can only point out that much of what has recently passed for theology of the priesthood in the Church has been little more than religious commentary on a present social situation. Some recent writing, and many places in the Vatican Council documents, are leading theological consideration back to its sources. In this book, we have given the word "priest" its present usage in church life, because we had to start from a present social situation. Writing from a theological viewpoint, we could point out that priesthood, in the Judaeo-Christian tradition, is a community function exercised by all who are called together by God to be his witnessing people.

Moses, when he came down from Sinai to speak to the people, passed on to them God's message: "Listen, then, to my voice, and keep your covenant with me; and I, to whom all the earth belongs, will single you out among its peoples to be my own. You shall serve me as a royal priesthood, as a consecrated nation" (Exodus 19:5–7). This theme linking the covenant with the whole priestly people is taken up several times in the New Testament writings; Peter writes: "You are a chosen race, a royal priesthood, a consecrated nation, a people God means to have for himself" (I Peter 2:9). This original linking of priesthood with people and covenant seems to be a rather neglected area of theology; the "priesthood of the laity" received strong emphasis in the Reformation, but its interpretation was often in terms of every man before God rather than in terms of community and covenant. Among Roman Catholic theologians, the community concept of priesthood and of covenant was neglected until recent times; priesthood was seen almost exclusively in terms of the clergy. Even with the welcome emphasis on group priesthood in the Vatican Council, theologians seem cautious in working out the implications of this in church life. If priesthood is to be seen basically in terms of community, of covenant, and of "koinonia" or shared fellowship, the theological function of the clergy will need reinterpreting, with a new style of liturgy and of common life in the Church to give something more than a token expression of the reality of communal priesthood.

The other neglected stream of theological thought on priesthood which is of interest in a book of this kind is the strong emphasis on the unique, final and determinative priesthood of Christ. This is proclaimed in the Epistle to the Hebrews with no uncertain voice; here again, theologians generally seem to be unwilling to move out of the present social situation of priesthood in the Church to tell us that none of us, really, are priests at all. It may well be that the early Christians, in avoiding any word meaning priest in referring to the officers and ministers of their community, were expressing their deep sense of belief in Christ as the final and definitive priest for mankind. Those of us who write from a social situation may well hope that the theologians will explore the authentic meaning of priesthood, in Christ, in the whole group of his followers, and in their group leaders. It seems that much clarification of the meaning in depth of this religious experience is necessary to help shape the role of the Catholic clergy in days to come.

12: ON THE PRIEST
AS BELIEVER / *a dialog*
about priests in crisis

After coming to a reasonable end point of this book, it seemed to me that if I were to be true to what I had written I should have some reaction, some feedback on this book as a communication. So I sent the draft of it to Doctor John Mackey, a priest who has been a friend to me for thirty years. I knew him as an excellent critic and as a scholar of wide competence in the fields touched on in this book. After he had read the draft we sat together one long afternoon and talked about it.

His detailed criticisms were useful and have, I think, helped to make this book more readable and alive. He attacked me for reading too many books and for borrowing the jargon of the sciences: "Your mind hasn't had time to get away from the technical terminology. This book doesn't come through to me as your real self, as your other books did. It's still full of dysfunctions, malfunctions, psychic energies and committed Christians —you communicate best just by being your real self, and saying what you want to say without the technicalities." So now the book, as you see it, has been shorn of most of its impressive obscurities.

During this discussion I had a tape recorder going so that I could make later corrections. We went on to talk about our overall impression of the book as a message. This led us on to discuss the role of the priest in a way which has not come through in this book. This was a live conversation between old friends; when I listened to the tape later on, I realized that its live quality was something I could not hope to catch in usual book style. So we decided to transcribe the taped conversation just as it was.

I should emphasize that this does not involve John Mackey in any responsibility for my opinions and for what I have written. He appears here as a critic; he has shown that he is quite capable of writing his own books. Here, then, is how our discussion went.

John: Is this tape recorder still going? You know, one of the things I thought you didn't do in your book is to say what a priest was—or at least, this didn't come through to me. You said how he operates as a social functionary. . . .

David: What I wanted to do, is to see the priest as a social person and to avoid entering into a theological discussion of what a priest is.

John: I don't think you can divorce the two very well, unless you specifically delineate this, but you don't seem to do this very clearly. After all, the Church is going to remain the Church, and it is going to have priests; you seem to finish up your book by saying that there aren't going to be any priests because their social functions are no longer relevant.

David: There may not be any full-time priests, professional priests as we know them. Maybe I should make this distinction more clearly.

John: I feel that you should. You can't just talk about priests without delineating your area, as Fichter does in his studies. He says: "I'm saying nothing about the theology of priesthood, I'm looking at this man, in this community, functioning in this way." What you have done is to concentrate on all the secondary functioning of a priest—his function as cult leader is hardly mentioned. If Christianity remains, there will continue to be someone who is operating as priest. He may not be a counselor, a moral instructor or a preacher, but he is going to be cult leader.

David: I certainly had this in mind in the latter part of the book—this is the only sure thing you can say about the essential function of priesthood in the Church. Someone sent me this article of Monsignor Illich, and he was speculating about the disappearance of the clergy as a full-time profession. I feel that there are a lot of trends which point in this direction, and this brings us back to what is the irreplaceable function of the priest—as you say, it is precisely that of cult leader, which is a one-hour-a-week job. So there's no reason why priesthood can't be combined with another vocation. The French worker-priest idea was a direct experiment on these lines; it wasn't particularly successful for a lot of social and political reasons. . . .

John: This sort of thing won't come about by planning; it will happen. It's the way society will go.

David: It has already happened to a lot of us priests. It's happened to you, to me, to Tom, to half the priests I know in the States. We do a social job for the general community on an ordinary working basis, as teachers, counselors, community planners and administrators. We do this community work as committed Christians, and we preside over a Christian assembly at the weekend. Most of the crisis points I talk about in this book center round the concept of the priest as a full-time parish worker, social leader of a Christian community.

John: The early Church obviously operated on this other concept; the cult leader continued to go about his ordinary job.

David: Except for the few who were propagandists more or less full-time, like Paul. But the people he chose out as local leaders were fathers of families in the local community. He chose, as he said, the man who had brought up a decent family and had respectability as a natural base of leadership.

John: In terms of priests and their needs, I think you have to bring this out clearly. What comes through to me as a general impression is that you have taken all their social functioning, in counseling, management, teaching, in being experts in morals and theology, and have shown these as evaporating. You seem to leave the priest with nothing.

David: I did show that the priest can be a center point, a mediator, in communications—which gets right back to the central meaning of priesthood. This is really what the cult leader is.

John: You have to develop this more clearly. Knowing priests as we do, I feel that they are under enough tension as it is. They're caught between the bishops, with their full priesthood, and the laity with their priesthood. They saw that the Vatican Council had only a quick look at the priest before it closed up. All of this had a profound psychological effect.

David: This is really what I am trying to say in the book. If priests are going to get out of this state of diffuse anxiety, we have to name the problem. Maybe there is so much describing of the problem in the book that this is what has come through to you as the dominant message.

John: What you have really done is to describe the problems around the priest; you haven't marked out the central problem of being a priest in a community. I think another chapter might bring this out. . . . Look at de Chardin: in his *Phenomenon of Man* he wasn't concerned with theology, he wasn't concerned with metaphysics. He was concerned with the problem of what man is in the universe. The whole accumulated evidence of science provides you with a problem in regard to man. In so many of his characteristics, he is identical with the animal creation. If he wasn't so obtrusive in nature, you could fit him in with some group or other of the vertebrates. But when you look at what he has actually done to the world, you have to assess man in terms of what he is to nature. He is like a butterfly in a chrysalis, he is constantly trying to break out of the cocoon of nature. When you put all this together, you haven't got a theological argument, or a philosophical one, but an argument of scientific differences which demand an explanation. Either we say, "We don't know—man is just a mystery," or we can conjecture from what man is to what he is possibly to be. This is de Chardin's argument; he doesn't give you an answer to the problem, he gives you a theory in terms of factual evidence. . . . It seems to me that you've got to do something of the same thing in regard to the priest. Look at him as he really is in society, with all his meaning. In this society in which we are, the priest has no being unless he has a theological being. What you must look at, cursorily but carefully, is a view of what the priest is if Christianity is Christianity. Call him cult leader, a communication mediator, a dispenser of the mysteries of Christ, what you like—but if Christianity continues, you must show the priest within it in his theological functioning. So far, your book seems to strip off all the layers of social functioning, like skinning an onion, and end up with nothing but tears—it leaves me with the suggestion that maybe Christianity is all wrong, a great mistake.

David: I don't find any real difference between the social and the theological dimensions of the functioning of the priest. Christianity is essentially a social phenomenon; it is God communicating himself socially. It is a message in persons and words, it has to do with people, community, love and fellowship. I have simply chosen to look at all this in the framework of the social meaning of our time, not in the traditional theological language.

John: This is fair enough. But all this, after all, isn't the real problem about priests today. The basic problem which is facing all priests is not the question of their social dysfunction, to use your favorite word, but their theological relevance. If there was suddenly, per impossible, a revelation that Christianity wasn't true after all, most of the priests would pack their bags, get a cosy little job, and go off happily to the grave along with the rest of voiceless humanity. I feel that their central problem is one of unexpressed doubts as to whether Christianity is true, true in a theological sense, not merely valid in a social sense. It's the question, "Is man made for judgment, or isn't he?" Or the more personal question, "Is there life after death or isn't there?"

David: "Is it meaningful to speak about God?"

John: And "Is it meaningful to speak about man?"

David: I think Leslie Dewart, in *The Future of Belief*, says that the question isn't whether God exists, but whether it means anything to speak about him. It's no use being able to prove that God exists or that Christ is his son unless this means something to people—otherwise you have a message without a meaning.

John: You've been reading McLuhan. I really don't agree with this. In one sense, yes, but I don't think this is what you're meaning.

David: What I do mean is that the whole of Christianity is a message—that Christ is the Word of God to man—that in the person, the life, the death and resurrection of Christ there is a communication.

John: What sort of communication? Is it a communication of man to man, or of God to man?

David: Both, I suppose. Certainly of God to man. When we use this phrase, the Word of God, about the scripture or about the person of Christ, we mean that God is saying something to man, and God is calling me, in this scripture and in this man and in the brotherhood of his followers.

John: Right.

David: This has to be validated, then, in terms of being understandable to man. The question of people like Dewart and Harvey Cox, "Is it meaningful to speak about God?" seems to me to be the right question. It is in this sense that I would ask, "Is God dead?" When I ask this question, I am not inquiring about some objectivity outside our personal experience, but I am asking whether this way of speaking is dead as a way of communication, like the pony express, or the . . . .

John: Let me put it this way. You seem to be saying, "Is the concept of God useful to the progress of man?" You imply that if it is not useful, let's get rid of it and just talk about man.

David: If we look seriously at man, we may find some word, some concept, which will really communicate to us as an absolute value.

John: This is fine—an open future?

David: I have a quotation here from Schillebeeckx which I used recently; he was speaking at a seminar in Toronto the other day. He says: "The Christian revelation, in the form in which it has been handed down to us, clearly no longer provides any valid answer to the questions about God asked by the majority of men today. It would also appear not to make any material contribution to modern man's meaningful understanding of himself in this world and in history." [1]

John: This I don't believe.

[1] Edward Schillebeeckx, speaking at Theologo '67 in Toronto, reported in *New Zealand Tablet*, September 13, 1967.

David: It was you who wanted theology.

John: You've just found one who fits your argument.

David: What seriously struck me about this quote is that the questioning of belief, which, you rightly say, is at the root of the clergy crisis, is right in among the theologians. It's not just the dumb ones among the priests who are having doubts, it's the clever people—particularly the clever people.

John: Sure. This is what is upsetting the dumb ones. But this, to me, isn't any problem.

David: It is to me. This loss of faith is important—the priest is nothing if he is not a believer. If there is a lack of personal and group confidence at this central point, it affects everything they do. I point out in this book that the clergy are suffering from a loss of meaning in their social functioning, that they have inherited a number of social functions which are going obsolete—where they are surviving, they are creaking. This may be the outward form of the same problem you talk of, because the two are deeply connected. The priests see going out of vogue a lot of the old functioning which they treasured because they were practical social expressions of their central functions as ministers of cult and preachers of the word. This contributes a lot to their general malaise and confusion.

John: But this is because they have never thought theologically. You know what we've often said before—what seminaries turned out are not theologians but technicians, people who were able to fix the spiritual plumbing. Now the plumbing is undergoing a radical technological transformation, and their technical skills are no longer applicable. . . . The theologians are thinking about the same problem, but they're not thinking of it in terms of technical skills, because that's not their field. They are thinking of the basic problem, which is man. The mystery, after all, is man; the mystery is not God. God is perfectly open to himself, has no doubts or wonders about himself. The mystery of man is

"What is he for? Is he for time or for eternity?" And we haven't any answer to that, all we have are presumptions. We have a whole concurrence of crossing points; but man's basic experience is that he is born and he dies, and that's it! He's definitely not satisfied with this as an answer. Then Christianity comes with a message that the tomb's open, open physically, in the real terms of the human person and his survival after death. So this is the function of the priest, to tell him that the tomb is open. And if this isn't true, then there's no relevance in the question of God, and no relevance in the question of the priest.

David: You seem to be linking the question of God and the question of immortality very closely.

John: That's right. Someone asked me the other day what is the whole basis of religion. I said that it's the question of man's mortality and immortality. If man has no immortality, then you can forget about God, and then you haven't any theological problem, only problems of humanism.

David: I would say, from my reading of the modern theologians, that the area of their doubt is particularly this one of immortality. They are very hesitant about life after death.

John: I think they're wrong on this. Otherwise, it seems to me, what you're doing to theology is that you're reverting right back to the social function of religion in the old empire—seeing religion as the cement of social solidarity. The early Christians had a different idea—new life that goes on through death and after—and it was for this that they died. If they died wrongly, fine. But it seems to me that they had the crucial question. If there is no life beyond the tomb, David my boy, we're not only out of business, we've been fooled! As St. Paul said.

David: So it looks as if we should get busy refining our idea of immortality if the new roles of the priest are to have genuine meaning. How can a man live on after death? This is what the priest must speak about to modern man, in some language that he can understand. Not in terms of harps and flowers—though poetry is often as good a way as any to express the deeper truths about man; it only worries those literal-minded people who can't appreciate the different styles in which messages can be presented . . . like people who feel that Shakespeare is not relevant because he's not scientific.

John: The real point for the priest is that man really lives on. The other popular idea of the theologians, and I think this is from Cullman, that the promise of scripture is resurrection of the body and not immortality—this I won't have at all.

David: That's hard to get around. After all, it was the resurrection of the body that the early Christians were so excited about.

John: I believe in the resurrection of the body. What I say, is that in terms of the center of consciousness, me, what I anticipate at death is not losing it, even for a time, but entering into it more fully. After death I'll be more fully myself than I've ever been. This full knowledge of myself and of what I am will reach its culmination in the resurrection of my body. This, I feel, is the center of the Christian message. This is what being a priest is all about.

David: In the medieval philosophy which we studied, this was all easy enough to say. We had our neat distinction of body and soul; we distinguished time and eternity. So the question of a time lag didn't bother us. These millions of years which might go on from our death until the end of the world might be experienced as a moment or two, since after death, entering into the realm of God, we came into a different time zone, a different way of experiencing transition. As long as I like to think to myself in these neat distinctions, I have no problem; when I try to explain all this to some modern intellectual, I have no message that he can understand.

John: I'm talking about the reality that is behind the message of the priest, not its language form. When Christianity first began to preach itself, it said that God has spoken to man, that he has revealed something of the mystery of man. Its basic facts are that Christ is the Word of God, that man becomes the child of God who can enter the same process of glorification that Christ went through—his cross and resurrection. . . . The early Christians went around saying this, and it took on. It fitted nicely with a lot of other things that were going on in men's minds, and so people began to ask questions. Now Dewart is right in this: the only way in which you can ask or answer questions is in terms of conflict with the view of reality which you have. This view of reality is mediated to you through the culture in which you have grown up, so your question is in relation to this culture view and the conflict you experience. . . . The person who answers you also belongs to the same cultural situation, so he can only use the same cultural tools. What the early Christians used, of course, were the technical tools of Greek philosophy. Now we don't look at the same sort of universe that the Greeks saw, the technical tools we use are different—and we have our great problem of relevance. So it doesn't worry me a bit, and it shouldn't worry priests, that the theologians are doing all this questioning and doubting. I don't care where they get to, or what words they find to use; but if they get lost in the situation, I don't intend to be lost personally. For me the reality is clear; it is the reality of man, the reality of my real and continuing self. Even though man still remains a mystery.

David: As you say, man remains the mystery. But because of this, God is a mystery to him, and this poses a huge problem to the priest of today who has to speak about God.

John: The only mystery about God is in the question, "Is he a reality, or isn't he?" And the message that the priest has is that he is the reality towards which man tends. If God is not real, then he is not the God of which the Bible speaks. If Christianity happens to be just a kind of concealed social program, I'm not particularly interested in it.

David: Nor am I. I could think of easier ways of having a social program. The problem as I see it is one of language.

John: It's a problem of how language relates reality. If you see only the problem of linguistics, you can get into the situation where linguistically you are left with nothing.

David: This is where some of the theologians are. If you can dig through what they're saying, they seem rather to be at a nothing point.

John: This doesn't worry me a bit.

David: It means to me that I have to look at the realities I see, and try to relate them to some relevant way of thinking and believing about Christ, and about God, and about life after death.

John: If you see these as real, then we are believers together. But Christ and God and immortality must be real—not just poetic images of social reality, not just mental projections, not just hope fulfilment, but things which exist in an ordinary sense of reality, ontologically. These are apprehended by us dimly; but they came out of history and hit us and said, "This is what man is for." That is why the way man lives with man, as community, must reflect these realities. They are vitally important for social communication and the upbuilding of human community, precisely because man must reflect the faith that ultimate reality is a community of loving. This is the meaning of God, this is what we mean by the Trinity, that God is not cold implacable reason. This is what Christianity did with philosophy; it shifted the emphasis from the explanation of why things are, to a demand that things should be different, and precisely because the source is a community of love. If this isn't so, and I have no vital relationship to that community of love in my span of life, then I'm just not interested.

David: Well, I would go with you on all this, I think.

John: But it is just this which doesn't come through in your book. It is because God is a community of love that there must be a great reform of the lack of communication in the Church, and the righting of injustices, and all the other things that you speak of; the Church must be a community of love, and the priests' striving must be to achieve this, so that the Church is a message to man. What comes through to me about the book is a concern with the things at hand, and an unconcern with otherworld realities. But the priest's task as cult leader is precisely to preach this thing we have been talking about. If he doesn't preach this, he can be the most efficient administrator, he can be the most polished liturgist, the finest counselor, and not a priest.

David: I agree. That is one of the things I am really trying to say in this book. This is where I feel a lot of priests are going wrong. They are simply going off to become psychologists and sociologists and planners and management experts. I think that many of them are not relating all this new knowledge and expertise to the real question of being a priest—they are living two disconnected lives. . . . Coming back to love again, you say that the striking message about God is that he is a community of love, a Trinity. This is an interesting commentary on the meaning of loving, that it involves three, not two. The great urge in personality psychology at present is man's quest for identity and meaning. There's a kind of metapsychology developing, a psychology about the meaning of man. We have looked experientially at man and human development and mental diseases and therapy and counseling, and now we are prepared to philosophize about man. This is what all the great psychologists do in their old age.

John: It's just what the logicians did in the Middle Ages. The only material we have to work on is human material; the only tools man has, as Dewart rightly says, are what his culture gives him. If all you've got is a logical framework, as they had in the Middle Ages, then this is what you use. In our day, we have, as you say, the empirical findings of the sciences of human behavior, so you start working on this in a metapsychological way. Because this is the unending quest of man, the search for wisdom.

David: This is where the priest of today has to formulate his message if it is going to have any relevance. To me, it seems that we should be able to do this, because all the answers, tentative as they are, that the metapsychologists and the metasociologists are arriving at, are formulated in terms like love, truth, identity and community, the same basic concepts which you find in the Bible.

John: And which you will find in the medieval philosophers. It's the same mystery of man. You read de Chardin, and you find that he is doing the same thing; what he has done is to use the material of the physical sciences, not the social sciences.

David: Still, what is there about loving that makes it immortal? We should be able to get some clues. . . .

John: Loving isn't immortal. What is characteristic about loving, I would say, is that it is loving which awakens the hunger for immortality. This is where man has always found himself. Once he starts loving, he cannot be satisfied with death. If you are truly in love, you don't want it to stop. If you're making money, you can retire and adapt yourself to a change. Things like making money or teaching are functional proficiencies. Loving is not; you can acquire a functional proficiency in sexual behavior, but loving itself is not functional. It is an extrapolation of the personality; it is a communication of the mystery of person to person. Person opens up to person the mystery of the depths of his own being. Once one actually begins to love, one feels that this must go on.

David: This is what convinces many people about immortality. Talk to a man who has loved very deeply someone who has just died, and you find that he can't conceive that this has suddenly and forever ended. There must be some link between this natural fact and the message of a priest that the Christian promise is of entering through death into a life of intensified loving, in the community of the Trinity.

John: I haven't much problem with this. Basically I have seen God as subsistent love. The only problem is why we have to go through the difficulties of this life to enter into this love. Original sin is the answer, not a very reasonable one, and I don't like it as an explanation. However, you come up against the difficulty that man must have the freedom to love, that this is his dignity.

David: You might see this life as an apprenticeship in loving.

John: No, I can't. The conditions for loving don't really operate in this life; you have to fight for it all the time. We're up against the brute facts of man's existence and experience, and how this generates love is one of the mysteries. Historically speaking, I would say that the only communities that have generated any full sense of what love is are the Christian communities. Everything that our modern world wants in terms of the good life, based on the scientific expertise of Europe, has grown up in and through Christianity. I know it is impossible to show any causal relationship. But every other community has known love only at the primitive family level; it has never expressed itself in any wider social structures than the family or small tribe. Every other community structure has been typically a power structure; it is only the Christian West that has thrown up the idea that the power structure must be used for the good of all.

David: Original sin doesn't cause me any difficulty. We're all very conscious of the way in which, by being born into a particular family and society and culture at any given moment, we inherit a web of human evil and frustration and limitation.

John: But why don't we come immediately into what seems to be the proper condition of man, what I think will be the final condition of all men. I feel that hell is going to be a lonely place, hard to get into. One or two may manage it, but they won't be the social misfits, but rather the Doctor Faustus figures, who know what the crucial decision is, as far as we can know it in these conditions, but who persist in making it.

David: The only sin, really, is the decision not to love.

John: True. . . . Now I've got you all confused in a theological phantasmagoria, far removed from those good social functions of the priest which you write about. Yet this, I think, is the essence of our discussion, because this is what being a priest is all about. The priest is a believer, a man with a message. This should come out in your book.

David: I have the feeling that this is another book, not the one I've written. I can bring some of these emphases more into light, certainly. But really, this is a book about the priest as seen through the light of the social sciences, as a social functionary within the social structures which I have experienced, the English-speaking communities. If I throw any light on the priest's faith as a believer, or on his theological meaning, it is by accident. I think one has to be honest to a purpose in writing; I have seen so much "religious sociology" which is poorly concealed preaching that I'm very conscious of a need to be true to my tools. I hope this book is a useful thing for me to do, and, I hope, for some to read. I have tried simply to use the tools I have learnt through the social sciences to throw light on a present social situation within the whole community.

John: I couldn't agree more. That bit on communication, particularly, is good and illuminating. But this is what I was getting at: the overall impression seemed to be an undermining of the meaning of what it is to be a priest. If this is how you feel, fine! But it is not how I feel. I agree with your social analysis, but it seems incomplete. If you simply want to do a neat piece of social study on the priest and his changing role, you've done it! But if you have a concern for the priests who are going to read it, you have to be prepared to come out of your academic framework. You can not only show what priests are going through in terms of social crisis and loss of social identity, you can actually help them go through it by taking proper note of their irreplaceable and continuing theological function. You don't have to enter into a theological discourse, simply to recognize the wider universe of significance in which the priest should be operating. If he is not operating in this wider frame of meaning, he is a social parasite.

David: I think I see what you mean . . . another short chapter, perhaps?

John: Yes, show what the basic Christian promise, message, kerygma, really is; show in these terms what a priest is. Show what history has done to this, where we have come to, and where the priest might go from here.

13: ON THE MEANING
OF CRISIS / and the risk
of caring

Our view of the social function of the priest remains incomplete
unless we see him as a believer, as a God-centered man, as a
symbol of Christ. Our societies, with all their ambiguities, are
very much what the Jewish-Christian tradition has made them.
Although many intelligent people in them prefer to formulate
social aims and theories in humanist rather than religious terms,
this is a humanism which has largely grown out of the Western
religious tradition.

The religious functionaries of our societies have been the
focus of a deeply formative influence on our way of thinking
about the human person, about freedom and justice, about community, and about loving. The Catholic priest—and, of course,
all the other Christian and Jewish leaders who are not the direct
concern in this book—has always stood in our society as a
meaning-man, the man with a message. Often his message is
distorted, misunderstood or rejected. But even the distortion
and rejection has been formative. Western agnosticism and
atheism are not rejections of animism, Buddhism or Taoism,
but of Christianity. And not even of Christianity as a whole,
but, in a selective way, only of those biblical or medieval images
and formulations which are felt to be irrelevant.

THE PRIEST AS BELIEVER

Within this framework of belief and unbelief, the priest is still a human being with a personal belief system. Along with all other men, he is engaged in a search for belief, for a personal place to stand, for a structure of values and of reality which will give meaning for him, and will relate him to the other men of his society. In this common search with his fellowmen, he is involved in their tension between personal initiative and conformity, and, like them, he reacts in terms of his own psychological growth and makeup, and in terms of the general and specific social situation in which he finds himself.

Because he is a priest, he is personally committed to belief in the Christian message and tradition, and faces the continuing task of making this immediate and relevant for his own life. In him as a person is played out the drama of updating which this book has considered on the larger scale. In a more stable society, living in a Church where movement is slow, he might easily have been content with the wisdom handed on to him from the past, and his area of personal belief may have been relatively free of tension and insecurity. Living in the world and Church of today, he finds that the very familiar securities of the past are themselves involved in the tensions of change.

Over and beyond this crisis of change and newness which the priest shares as a believer with many others in his society, he is involved in a crisis of social belief precisely because he is a believing-man of our society at the moment. Because of his central role of guarding meaning and value in a society of Jewish-Christian tradition and sentiment, the priest is at the center of a belief crisis which is social as well as directly religious. Every society, as it makes its great decisions, must formulate and reformulate for itself its reason for being, and the meaning of its ideals. Our Western societies have found their reasons and ideals very largely in their religious traditions and in the humanism which has grown out of these traditions. As these traditions and ideals face the challenge of all the change which this book has discussed, it is not only the churches, but our societies themselves which are going through a crisis of meaning and value. The credibility gap which we speak of when we listen to political leaders is much deeper than any doubt of their integrity as persons; it is a projection of doubt in the foundation beliefs of our social system.

The clergyman is one of our society's many guardians and interpreters of these foundation beliefs. As we have seen happening in the history of the Church, these social beliefs attract to themselves the dominant social and political urges and forces of the moment, which form a kind of alliance with them. Through modern communication we are more than ever conscious of the way in which high-minded social ideals and constitutional principles are distorted and adulterated by this alliance with the acquisitive, aggressive and defensive social drives of the moment. This often involves the clergy in an uneasy fellowship with militarists, imperialists, financiers, patriots and politicans of all shades of opinion and degrees of integrity; priests, because of their social position, are expected to back up the policeman and the present social order and to bless the soldiers and their weapons.

Bob Dylan sings a sad little song called "With God on Our Side" which expresses the cynical disbelief that is disturbing much of American society. He tells how Americans were able, in all their wars, to claim God on their side while they were killing the Indians and the Mexicans, shooting one another, and raining bombs on the Germans and the Japanese. Pete Seeger sings of the same cynicism when he asks his child, "What did you learn in school today?" and questions the values of justice and order in a non-sharing and self-satisfied society. Those who find the God in which this society trusts somehow unbelievable may find their atheism easily spreading to those social ideals of democracy, of social justice, of due process, of peace, and of love for all men, which are smeared with the same grime of human history. The priest, as living representative of the tradition behind these ideals, finds his role the object of the same cynical atheism. He, like many politicians and administrators, finds himself straddling a credibility gap, with nowhere to stand. When meaning has been lost, a meaning-man is voiceless with no words left to use.

While the priest is left wondering, the whole shape of our society as a way of being together is under rapid change. McLuhan sums up this change in his dictum: "The medium is the message." He stresses that it was not what printing said, but rather the very fact of printing that was the vehicle of vast social change; he points out that it is today's instant electronic communication which is the message of change to our society.

> After three thousand years of specialist explosion and of increasing specialism and alienation in the technological extensions of our bodies, our world has become compressional by dramatic reversal. As electrically contracted, the globe is no more than a village. Electric speed in bringing all social and political functions together in a sudden implosion has heightened human awareness of responsibility to an intense degree. . . . The aspiration of our time for wholeness, empathy and depth of awareness is a natural adjunct of electric technology. The age of mechanical industry that preceded us found vehement assertion of private outlook the natural mode of expression. Every culture and every age has its favorite model of perception and knowledge that it is inclined to prescribe for everybody and everything. The mark of our time is its revulsion against imposed patterns. We are suddenly eager to have things and people declare their beings totally. There is a deep faith to be found in this new attitude—a faith that concerns the ultimate harmony of all being.[1]

This new expression of faith, springing from a new and more immediate vision of reality and of human relationships, has

[1] Marshall McLuhan, *Understanding Media* (New York: McGraw-Hill, 1964) , p. 5.

been the background concern throughout this book as we have looked at the changing role of the priest. The social-religious myths which supported a past order and the wealth and power which this order gave to the few are no longer viable. Even the national myths that supported the wars of our time are eroding fast as McLuhan's world village takes shape. This change is not just in how we live together, but especially in how we believe together. Divided and competing churches no longer make any sense. The managed information and the pious platitude with which president and cardinal, general and pastor, satisfied their people in the past, is no longer viable when it must be said in instant view of the sitting rooms of the world. The ugly facts of killing and hunger, of poverty and squalor, of greed and non-sharing, of censorship and repression, no longer can be hidden quietly away lest they disturb the faith and security of the people. The priest, the man who was the traditional guardian of social beliefs, is now deeply involved in the search for new ways to make life credible, new ways of believing together.

THE NEW NET GOES FISHING

I am writing this sitting in the spring sunshine on the bank of a river where it flows into the Pacific. A group of Maori boys are fishing with an old dragnet just below me at the outlet. As they haul in the net, it breaks apart in the surf, and I am listening to their cries of dismay. I have just reminded them of one of the ancient proverbs of our island people: *Ka pu te ruha, ka hao te rangitahi*—the worn-out net is laid aside, and the new net goes fishing. There are times when the old, the comfortable and the friendly things of our life are past their use, and we must start with something new.

The first Christian priests were chosen on an occasion just like this one I have been watching. The net, which we now use as a symbol of wide communication of meaning, was also used by

Christ as a symbol of the work to which he was calling his fishermen in Galilee; he said to them, "follow me; come and I will make you into fishers of men" (Matthew 4:19). The gospels are full of stories of nets and fish based on this symbolism.

As new nets of human meaning and relationship, new modes of human communication, transform our societies with their message, the priest, if he is to stay as a believer in the Church and in his society, must go fishing with the new net. As a leader of Christian believers, his fidelity is to the message and person of Christ, whom he sees as the key figure of the religious and social tradition we have been discussing. He must, too, as a faithful believer, see Christ as the key figure in the ongoing crisis of faith that is our experience. But if Christ is to be this key figure for men of today, the priest must express this in the meaning of today. He must be prepared to set aside the worn-out net, and go fishing with the new one.

Priests, in this crisis, seem to move in two divergent directions. Some still see their fidelity as believers as an urge to preserve all that is best in the past; they see faith in Christ and in the message of the Bible as a storehouse of wisdom for men and societies. Their concern is that, in an atmosphere of rapid change, some of this may be lost. Greatest among their concerns is the sight of the number of priests who seem to be moving enthusiastically into change, who see Christ calling man into a better future rather than urging him to preserve the values of the past.

These two groups of priests, naturally enough, see the Church in quite a different way. The first group see the task of the Church primarily as one of preservation, of "saving souls" from the evils of the time and from evils in the future. The second group sees the task as the "building of the kingdom of God," with a strong orientation to the future. They feel that, in the continuing presence of Christ, God is authenticating the personal growth and the social development of men, calling them to grow in community and common care to be the people of God in love and brotherhood. This division, like most of the human situations described in this book, is typical of the different ways in which men structure their experience and their hopes; most human groups will find an internal division along these conservative and progressive lines.

One of the consequent differences among priests is in the very concept of their function as believers and leaders of a believing community. Those whose orientation is towards past values and their preservation will continue to look at past formulations for clear answers to the questioning men of today in their search for faith and meaning. They will see, in the Bible, in the Christian creeds, in the decrees of church councils, in encyclicals of popes, and in "the way things have always been done," the source of security and certainty to live by. They will experience change and evolution in human and church affairs as disturbing this proper order to some extent, perhaps also as a mild concession to the times. When this concession is authenticated by authority, as in the Vatican Council, priests of this type will usually accept change gracefully enough, since here the change is perceived as secondary to the element of unchanging authority.

Priests whose orientation is to the future see their role as Christian believer and leader very differently. They see faith as a continuing search for meaning and relevance, and see themselves with their people as fellow searchers rather than as answer men. They find in the Bible, in the creeds and encyclicals, challenges for this search rather than ready-made answers. They see the recent Vatican Council as a starting point rather than as an achievement. They experience much of the present caution and use of authority by church leaders as a brake on an exciting and essential development.

Many priests, as always, will find themselves somewhere in between these two groups; there is usually something of both these attitudes in most of us. This ambiguity is an important element in the crisis situation this book has been describing. The fact that most priests feel that the positions at the extremes are untenable leaves them in an in-between position that is difficult to explain logically and difficult to espouse with any real enthusiasm. Crisis often seems to demand of us an either-or response; halfway solutions are often unconvincing and ineffective. In many ways the priest who stands uncertainly in the middle is subject both to the tensions of the conservative as he faces rapid change and the danger of his growing irrelevancy, and the tensions of the progressive as he realizes how easily he may be disowned by the people he wants to serve and by the authority system under which he lives.

THE PRIEST AS ATHEIST

We can see the priest as believer only when we see him also as unbeliever. Every belief we establish for ourselves puts us in the position of disbelieving in something else. Our system of disbelief is as important to us as our system of belief. This is all the more so since they often coexist in us; we are like the man in the gospels who pleaded with Jesus: "I believe, Lord, help my unbelief."

As a social and historical phenomenon, the whole Jewish-Christian tradition has been experienced not only as a new movement of common belief, but more strikingly, wherever it has made its driving impact on societies, as a movement of atheism and unbelief. From the time that the nameless god of the desert spoke to Moses, it was a movement marked by its practical atheism, its iconoclastic energy in proclaiming the death of the gods of men and of their societies. Its followers worshipped a god without a name and without a place, and his first demand was that the gods should be destroyed, that men must have no idols.

Through history, this has been a movement of protest against established orders and divinities. We see this vividly in the lives of the Jewish prophets, and in Christ rejecting all the expectations of his society to make his life and death a one-man demonstration of peace, love and reconciliation. We see it in Paul preaching in Athens to an unknown god, and in the labors of Christian missionaries to destroy, at times so needlessly, the gods of all men everywhere. Christianity is the belief to destroy man's religions, to break his idols and dethrone his gods. Many priests are seeing it today as a movement of protest against the social idols of our time; they are saying that the priest who is really to be a Christian must resign his comfortable position as guardian of the old social values. If he is truly a believer in Christ, they say, he must lead the marchers against the dying gods of our social order, must pour out blood on the idols of war and hate.

Here is another of the crisis points of choice for the priest. How thorough and vigorous must he be in his atheism? Is it enough to say, "There is no god but the Lord, and him only shall we worship"? Is this a time to build up, or a time to break down? A time to cast away stones, or a time to gather stones together? A time to keep silence, or a time to speak? A time to love or a time to hate? A time for war, or a time for peace? (Ecclesiastes 3:1–9). Can the priest of today continue as the faithful servant of society, its dedicated meaning-man, trying gradually to purify its values and ideals from within? Can he move along quietly, building slowly and surely, careful not to break down what has been built up, and not disturbing the peace and good order of Church and society? This is the carefully limited atheism which many priests choose.

Or must he, even to be a traditionalist, faithful to the message and drive of the Bible, resign in effect his traditional role as the guardian of social values and faithful servant of what is? Must he choose the way of radical Christian belief and of energetic atheism? Can he really leave the urgent proclamation of the death of the idols of our time to others? Can he leave the joyful celebration of love and peace to the beatniks and the hippies?

And the song about the dignity and freedom of man to Pete Seeger and Joan Baez and Bob Dylan? And the proclamation of justice and of the new world to the Marxists?

Many, especially among younger priests, see these questions as the point of their personal crisis of belief and unbelief. They are saying that all the gods and idols of our societies are false, and that many of them are at home in the Church. They are saying that there is no god but the nameless one who will make his presence in man, as he did fully and finally in Christ, the model man of the new time. They are proclaiming his message that the only meaning of God, for men and society, is light in the darkness, love for a brother man, food for the hungry of the world, drink for the thirsty, freedom that truth makes for us, peace which is our inheritance.

I have tried to describe this tension among priests vividly, because this is how it presents itself, as an urgent crisis of belief and unbelief. It is not for me, in this book, to be telling priests where they must stand on these issues, but rather to describe what I see in the crisis situation of the priests of today. Every priest must find a standing place for himself.

THE PRIEST AS CULT LEADER

We have seen that it is when the priest presides as leader of a group of Christians in worship that his meaning and identity as a priest becomes clear. Here he is the cult leader, both the man of tradition and the man of the future; here his personal aims and choices are dominated by the fact that he is leader of a ritual group. It is the belief of the whole group which colors and determines this experience. This belief is that the group are gathered in the name of Christ, and that he becomes present once more among them in a particularly vivid way.

It is important, for the purpose of this book, for us to see clearly what the priest is on this occasion, for it is the key of his social function. It is to this function that our discussion has had to come back time and again, for the whole function of the priest in a society is related to the worship experience. Men everywhere have felt the need to ritualize their sense of the divine and to celebrate the salvation history of their people in joy, song and thanksgiving. In the Christian order, as we have seen, the ordained priest presides over the priestly people to proclaim with them the message of God in Christ, to proclaim in this believing group the joy and freedom symbolized in the death and resurrection of Jesus who is present again in the shared signs of food and drink.

Here the priest celebrates a peace demonstration, in memory of the demonstration of peace and reconciliation in the death and resurrection of the Lord Jesus.

Here the priest is a leader in joy and thanksgiving.

Here the priest teaches men to join hands and to share what they have.

Here the priest celebrates a love festival.

Here the priest leads men in a freedom song.

Here the priest tells men that the time for hate is gone, that now is the time for love.

It seems clear enough, from traditional as well as progressive views, that it is the cult of peace, freedom, love and human reconciliation that is celebrated by the gathering of believing Christians in the presence of their Lord; this is the cult of which the priest is leader. There would be little argument among Christians about all this, however much discussion may go on about the proper words and ceremonial needed to express it.

The need for reform and renewal in this area of worship, so central to the priest's identity as a social functionary, becomes very evident when we go to a large city church some Sunday morning. The elements of belief and intention highlighted above will certainly be present; they will generally be experienced only in some wishful way, lost to the order of ordinary human experience. Somehow the traditional forms of ceremonial and prayer and preaching have so gathered the dust of the centuries that they no longer come alive as the vivid experience of meaning that we expect. It seems that men today are more likely to find this vivid and live meaning in peace demonstrations, freedom marches, love-ins, teach-ins and thanksgiving dinners; here in the South Pacific we marvel at the joy, grace and dignity of the natural social liturgies of the Polynesians and the interweaving of song, dance, oratory and festival meal which makes their social occasions the envy of a professional liturgist.

The lack of existential meaning and life in the ordinary worship experience of the priest with Roman Catholics is, finally, a moving expression of the crisis situation of the clergy, and of their urgent search for social meaning, identity and purpose. It is not surprising, in this sensed urgency, that many priests feel bound to step outside the formal structures of church obedience to make their own way of celebrating a living worship with an experimental group. For many of these priests who have spoken to me, there has been a genuine feeling that the task of creating this new and vital meaning is fully urgent for their own survival as priests and for the continuing faith of many of the people who worship with them. They have felt that the cautionary directives of pope and bishop are, for the moment, of much less weight and concern.

Some priests are quietly pointing to the old tradition of creative disobedience as the normal way, in history, for the reform of the Church and its structures, and are asking themselves, in relation to each of the crisis points outlined in this book, whether any real movement will come if priests wait around for someone in authority to authenticate their action beforehand. They point to the creative disobedience to authority which was a mark of Christ and his early followers, and which has been a quiet but strong element in the continuing life of the Church.

Most priests, on the other hand, find this attitude to liturgy and to other social crisis situations something quite wrong in a priest, and claim that renewal and reform can only come through obedience and good order. Here, then, is one of the practical points of crisis where the modern priest must choose a stand of personal meaning and dedication. Can life in the church, in the parish, in the city cathedral, the life and form of the clergy, and the present commitment to social reform, really go on basically unchanged, with the careful and moderate updating that the Vatican Council outlined? Or must some radical position become an essential part of being a Christian and of being a priest? "Men are born only to die, plant trees only to displant them. . . . Weep first, then laugh, mourn we and dance" (Ecclesiastes 3.2-4).

THE CONTINUING MEANING OF A PRIEST

This book is specifically about the changing aspects of the role of the priest in our culture. Perhaps these changing aspects may be highlighted if we do what our dialog suggested: look briefly at what seems to be continuous in the function of the priest.

The first Christians believed that the Jewish religious-social roles of prophet, priest and king found a definitive fulfillment in the person of Jesus. To them he was, finally and effectively, the prophet, priest and king of a new and liberated humanity. In accord with their Jewish tradition, they saw their own brotherhood as carrying on these roles in the name and spirit of Christ. Peter expressed this when he told them, "You are a chosen race, a royal priesthood . . . , a people God means to have for himself; it is yours to proclaim the exploits of the God who has called you out of darkness into his marvelous light" (I Peter 2:9).

They felt that they were witnesses, in the name and spirit of Jesus, of God's final and definitive message to mankind. This was a message of good news, proclaiming that in Christ man could find reconciliation and peace. It announced that his death was the final and sufficient love-offering for all time, the fulfillment of man's urge to offer sacrifice, to make a peace-offering for evil and alienation.

The Christians proclaimed that now, therefore, men must enter a way of loving and caring, that this was the meaning of brotherhood in Christ. They witnessed to the open tomb, to the way in which the love of Jesus had conquered death; they said that all who live in his love will live forever. They held celebrations of these events and this message, weaving into a thanksgiving ceremony elements of old Jewish tradition centering around the Passover meal. In this cultic celebration they reenacted the final Passover meal of Jesus and his followers and experienced his real presence once more among them.

Leadership in this proclamation and celebration fell to the twelve apostles and to those who became leaders in the local groups of Christians which sprang up around the Mediterranean. Although both witness and worship were strongly communal, they had authenticity through the accredited group leadership; the gathering of the faithful for liturgy came to have no validity without its presiding leader.

This seems to be the irreplaceable role of the priest in Christianity. He is a member of the believing and witnessing brotherhood, a "brother among brothers," sharing their common commitment. He is their accredited leader, the focus and voice of their communal priesthood in Christ. He presides over their assembly, and as cult leader gives authentic meaning to the liturgical proclamation of the good news, in which the presence of Christ is again shared in the Passover meal.

We have seen, in this book, how history grew around the priest. Because he was a leader in the growth and expansion of the Christian fellowship, he had a formative effect on the societies which grew up in the Western Christian tradition. And these societies, in the tensions of their growth, had their effect on the priest. His role took on many social forms, often only loosely related to his central function as witness and mediator. Some of these social functions have already long disappeared; others are now under discussion.

This book has considered the crisis of meaning and identity which relates to the priest's changing role. I have suggested that many of the social aspects of this role are obsolescent, and that this is a root cause of crisis, confusion and anxiety among priests. John Mackey, in our dialog, pointed to the crisis that affects the priest as believer, but this is not my central concern.

I have been concerned to point out that, while some of the historically conditioned social functions of the priest may be vanishing into irrelevance, priests might well be seeking new forms of church life which will give relevance to their essential role. This means a recognition of the meaning of this crisis; it demands openness in looking at their future. For priests, I feel that the future offers challenge and promise, as they search for a modern framework of meaning to give relevance to the message they bear.

This book's concern has been a social analysis of the present situation rather than a sketch of a likely future. However, I feel that the chapter on communications and the implications in following chapters provide a possible frame of modern meaning in which tomorrow's priest might find his relevance.

We looked at the whole brotherhood of Christians as a communications system, a living message to mankind, a group who live in love and care, in commitment to God's communication in Christ. The priest is one of this witnessing fellowship and most of what he does is an expression of that fact that he is a Christian. We speculated that most of the social forms which have made a distinction between the priest and the layman in the Church may well disappear. Priests may not be professionals, but rather Christians chosen to be leaders of witnessing groups because of their maturity and the dedicated quality of their service to men. The brotherhood of Christians may well become an outwardly oriented group, very little concerned with internal group problems and functions. It may have a wide variety of accredited functionaries working in partnership. Among these, there will be the distinctive role of the priest.

We conceive the priest as the center point of a communications net concerning itself with man at the level of ultimate meaning. We say that the priest is the center man or mediator of this net, with a traditional message and a modern relevance, at a point where he listens to man adaptively and mediates meaning and purpose. The priest may find that this field of function takes him wherever people are thinking seriously about the meaning of life and its human problems; it may take him wherever people have the urge to celebrate love and peace.

It may take him into unlikely places. It may not be in a suburban parish, or in a school, or in a church—it will more likely be where men are in conflict and where human affairs are in crisis. It will be wherever people are discussing their questions of destiny, identity and community; it may be here that the priest must come with a message which it is his task to make relevant to man's concerns. These concerns will center round the questions of truth and love, as people question, "Who am I?" "Where do we go?" and "How do we love?"

ON THE MEANING OF CRISIS

The central concept of this book, as its title indicates, is that of crisis. Crisis is a point of decision, a moment when the circumstances of life—of things, of people, of ourselves—bring us to a situation which cannot be allowed to go on aimlessly; it is a point where even to do nothing is itself a serious decision to make. Crisis is neither good nor bad in itself; we often experience it as a relief, as when a doctor tells us, during a long illness, that we have reached the point of crisis. Those who have worked with alcoholics will know how little they seem able to do, and how little others can do for them, before they experience crisis.

Priests seem to find it no easier than most people to admit crisis in their lives and in their profession; as most people, they tend to run away from it, to deny its existence, to hope that problems will go away before something has to be done about them. They are as likely as anyone to rationalize their life difficulties, to engage in the game of collusion by organizing to busy themselves about straw problems with easy solutions. The life of the clergy offers unusual opportunities for the use of busywork to hide real issues.

It seems a pity that this should be so, because it is precisely at the point of human crisis that the priest should stand. Crisis is an unescapable element in human existence and in the life of groups and societies; it is the point at which decision is difficult, urgent, challenging, frightening. We have seen throughout this book that it will normally be experienced in terms of anxiety, hope, confusion and hostility. For some, this is the inevitable road to lassitude, hopelessness and defeat; for others, it may be the way to hope, originality, spontaneity, freedom and responsibility. The first step on the way of hope is to admit the crisis in all its hard reality, to accept it with all its difficulty.

In the teaching stories of Christ in the gospels and in his own life, there are many instances of human crisis—of people finding themselves and losing themselves; finding their neighbor and being unwilling to care; going into risk and running away from it; being open to change and being closed to it. The New Testament shows us life in terms of real and personal issues, in terms of man leaving the security of the old and worn-out ways to venture into the new—into new life, new birth, new community, new being. It presents human experience to us in life or death terms, leading us to face crisis.

It is, then, precisely at the point of crisis that the Church, the witnessing and communicating group of those who believe and love in this way, should situate itself. It is here that the human community may need the message they carry, it is here that men may be willing to listen. If I want to be able to help my alcoholic friend, I must be around precisely when he comes to the point of crisis, or I am wasting my time. So too, if the Church and the priest are not present at the points of human crisis, at the time and the place where the difficult and agonizing decisions are being made in a man's life or in the life of the community, their message will not be heard. If the priest is too busy somewhere else, tending to a variety of uncritical affairs, he seems to be in the wrong place as a Christian witness; he is like a policeman polishing his desk while a riot is going on, like a fireman cleaning his helmet while the house is on fire, like a shepherd looking after the ninety-nine while one is lost, like a man running a comfortable city parish within a mile of the ghetto.

It is where human affairs are in crisis that the Church may find its meaning, may be able to serve as a communication system between one man and another, between one group and another; it is here that it may mediate between mankind and the ultimate symbols of human meaning, the final personal expression of love and truth and life. It is at these crisis points of personal and social experience that men come to the crossroads of argument and life-meaning, to the turning points of decisions, to the yes or no point of human and social relationships. It is at these points that risks will be taken or will be avoided, that dangers will be challenged or retreated from, that courage will be shown or defeatism confirmed; it is here that men will begin to live in hope or will drift on into despair, that some will come to love and some will fail to care. It is in crisis that faith is born.

Because this is so, the priest has a special need to see his own professional crisis clearly, to admit its reality, to communicate openly about it, to deal with it positively in terms of the life ideals which he carries as a message to others. There are, as we have seen in this book, many special difficulties, confusions and anxieties about the role crisis of the priest today, and no kind of optimistic idealism should be allowed to deny the reality of what we have discussed. Nor should any kind of helpless indifference lead to an attitude of not caring, of concluding that nothing is really going to be much help. I feel that the positive elements and movements which concerned the latter part of this book, and the many rich suggestions I have heard from priests, bishops, psychologists and sociologists in discussion, offer to this crisis situation a measure of hope for those who are willing to take the risk of caring.

BIBLIOGRAPHY

This is a selection of the books I have found interesting and useful while writing this book. It may be of use to those who are interested in further reading.

Abbott, Walter, editor, *The Documents of Vatican II,* New York: Guild Press, America Press, Association Press and Herder & Herder, 1966.

Bowers, Margaretta K., *Conflicts of the Clergy,* New York: Thomas Nelson & Sons, 1963.

Callahan, Daniel, *The Mind of the Catholic Layman,* New York: Charles Scribner's Sons, 1963.

Cox, Harvey, *The Secular City,* New York: Macmillan, 1965.

Dewart, Leslie, *The Future of Belief,* New York: Herder & Herder, 1967.

Eagleton, Terence, *The New Left Church,* Baltimore: Helicon, 1966.

Erikson, Erik H., *Insight and Responsibility,* New York: Norton, 1964.

———, *Identity and the Life Cycle,* New York: International Universities Press, 1959.

———, *Childhood and Society,* New York: Norton, 1950.

Fichter, Joseph H., *Priest and People,* New York: Sheed and Ward, 1965.

———, *Religion as an Occupation,* Notre Dame, Indiana: University of Notre Dame Press, 1961.

Freud, Sigmund, *An Outline of Psycho-analysis,* New York: Norton, 1949.

Godin, André, *The Pastor as Counselor,* New York: Holt, Rinehart and Winston, 1965.

Goldman, Ronald, *Readiness for Religion,* New York: Seabury Press, 1965.

———, *Religious Thinking from Childhood to Adolescence,* New York: Humanities Press, 1965.

Halmos, Paul, *The Faith of the Counsellors,* New York: Schocken, 1965.

Kavanaugh, James, *A Modern Priest looks at his Outdated Church,* New York: Trident Press, 1967.

Lynch, William, *Images of Hope,* New York: Mentor-Omega Books, 1966.

Maslow, Abraham, *Toward a Psychology of Being,* Princeton: Van Nostrand, 1962.

Monden, Louis, *Sin, Liberty and Law,* New York: Sheed and Ward, 1965.

Müller, Alois, *Obedience in the Church,* Westminster, Md.: Newman, 1966.

McKenzie, John L., *Authority in the Church,* New York: Sheed and Ward, 1966.

McLuhan, Marshall, *Understanding Media,* New York: McGraw-Hill, 1964.

Neal, Marie Augusta, *Values and Interests in Social Change,* Englewood Cliffs, N.J.: Prentice-Hall, 1965.

Novak, Michael, *Belief and Unbelief,* New York: Macmillan, 1965.

O'Neill, David P., *Priestly Celibacy and Maturity,* New York: Sheed and Ward, 1965.

———, *About Loving,* Dayton, Ohio: Geo. A. Pflaum Publisher, Inc., 1966.

Piddington, Ralph, *Malinowski and the Study of Man,* Wellington: Government Printer, 1965.

Pius XII, *Guide for Living, Addresses and Letters,* New York: McKay, 1958.

Rahner, Karl, *Bishops, Their Status and Function,* Baltimore: Helicon, 1964.

Robinson, John A. T., *On Being the Church in the World,* Philadelphia: Westminster, 1960.

Rogers, Carl, *On Becoming a Person,* Boston: Houghton Mifflin Co., 1961.

Rokeach, Milton, *The Open and Closed Mind,* New York: Basic Books, 1960.

Ryan, Mary Perkins, *Are Parochial Schools the Answer?* New York: Holt, Rinehart and Winston, 1964.

Slant Manifesto, Springfield, Ill.: Templegate, 1961.

Sprott, W. J., *Human Groups,* Gloucester, Mass.: Peter Smith, 1958.

Teilhard de Chardin, Pierre, *Divine Milieu,* New York: Harper & Row, 1960.

———, *The Phenomenon of Man,* New York: Harper & Row, 1959.

Tillich, Paul, *Theology of Culture,* New York: Oxford University Press, 1959.

———, *The Shaking of the Foundations,* New York: Charles Scribner's Sons, 1948.

White, Ralph K., and Lippitt, Ronald, *Autocracy and Democracy,* New York: Harper and Brothers, 1960.

Woodcock, George, *Anarchism,* Gloucester, Mass.: Peter Smith, 1963.

INDEX